HOME LIGHTING

By the Editors of Sunset Books and Sunset Magazine

Lane Publishing Co. • Menlo Park, California

About this book . . .

Whether you're planning your overall lighting needs, looking for effective solutions to specific lighting problems, or seeking information on basic electrical circuitry, this book will fill your needs.

The first section offers guidance in determining what levels of light you'll need, and where. A rundown of available fixtures and bulbs is included, as well as some up-to-date energy tips.

The 64-page middle section of color photographs presents an exciting variety of lighting applications for every room in your home—and for outdoors, too. You'll also find an easy way to try out your lighting ideas, as well as some plans for making your own lamps.

Finally, in the last section, you can learn how to wire it all together. A basic explanation of electrical circuitry is given, in addition to step-by-step instructions for changing and installing fixtures and adding switches and outlets.

For their professional guidance, thorough checking, and thoughtful support, we thank Paul Engelhart, Cliff Kramer, Richard Peters, and Fran Kellogg Smith.

Others who generously shared their lighting ideas, expertise, and examples include Dan Blitzer, Lightolier; Terry Campbell; Ed Cargill and Frank Mann, Stanford Electric Works; Charles Davis; Doug Herst, Peerless Lighting; Kenneth Lim; Luminae, Inc.; David Malman; Gary Mole and Ray Randall, Prescolite; Tim Morse, Casella Lighting; Ross Lighting Studio; Pam Seifert; Bruce Velick; Karen Viara, Sacramento Municipal Utilities District; and Randall Whitehead, Light Source.

Cover: Recessed eyeball fixtures work wonders in this slant-ceilinged living room. Four of the fixtures, lined up close to the wall on the right, bring out the texture of brick and send reflected light to the sitting area below. An adjustable pharmacy floor lamp beside the chair provides a movable reading light. Aimed at the step to the lower sitting level, a single eyeball fixture gives light for safe stepping. Shelves displaying a pottery collection are lighted by a series of the same adjustable fixtures. Architect: Charles Moore. Lighting design: Richard Peters. Photographed by Jack McDowell. Cover design by Zan Fox.

Editor, Sunset Books: David E. Clark

First printing October 1982

Library of Congress Catalog Card Number: 82-81371.

ISBN 0-376-01312-5.

Lithographed in the United States.

Photographers

Jack McDowell: 25 top, 35 left, 45 bottom. **Steve W. Marley:** 17, 18, 19, 20, 21, 22, 23 left, 24, 25 bottom, 25, 27, 28, 29, 31, 32, 33, 34, 35 right, 36, 37, 38, 39, 41, 42, 43, 44, 45 top, 46, 47, 49, 51, 52, 53, 54, 55, 56, 57, 58, 59, 60, 61, 62, 63, 64, 64, 66, 67, 68, 70, 71, 72, 73, 74, 75, 76, 77, 78. **Norman A. Plate:** 48. **Bill Ross:** 23 right.

Supervising Editor:
Maureen Williams Zimmerman

Research & Text:
Sarah S. Norton
Michael Scofield

Design & Photo Editor:
Roger Flanagan

Illustrations:
Bill Oetinger
Judy Wilson Lynn

CONTENTS

THE BASICS OF GOOD LIGHTING

PLACEMENT • FIXTURES & BULBS

Good lighting design has an elusive quality; when you walk into an effectively lighted room, your eyes sense that everything is easily visible, but you'll rarely remark, "What fantastic lighting!"

For our eyes don't see the light itself, of course, but the things on which it shines. Light serves as a silent partner in enhancing our surroundings.

Whether you feel that your home needs more light or you're planning lighting for a new house or addition, you'll find this book full of useful ideas, new and traditional, large-scale and small. We've tried to capture some of the elusive qualities of effective lighting design and to explain them in direct terms to guide you to more effective lighting.

Lighting consultants. Once you have some ideas in mind, you may want to contact a lighting consultant, either for advice or for a complete plan, depending on your project and your budget. In many larger cities there are firms that specialize in lighting design (look under "Lighting Consultants" or "Lighting Systems & Equipment" in the Yellow Pages).

Architects and interior designers may list lighting as a specialty. All three of these types of consultants usually belong to the Illuminating Engineering Society (IES). Stores and electrical supply houses dealing in lighting fixtures may have in-house consultants, too.

ELEMENTS OF LIGHTING DESIGN

An essential ingredient in lighting design is simple common sense. The best lighting designer is a problem-solver, determining where light is wanted and needed, and then putting it there with economy and flair. You can take the same approach using the following three main types of lighting.

Task lighting illuminates a particular area where a visual activity—such as reading, sewing, or preparing food—takes place. It's often achieved with individual fixtures that direct light onto a work surface. Task lighting can be the basis of a good lighting plan.

Accent lighting is similar to task lighting in that it consists largely of directional light. Primarily decorative, accent lighting is used to focus attention on artwork, to highlight architectural features, to set a mood, or to provide drama.

Ambient or general lighting fills in the undefined areas of a room with a soft level of light—say, enough to watch television by or to navigate safely through the room. Ambient lighting usually comes from indirect fixtures that provide a diffuse spread of illumination. Directional fixtures can also be aimed at a wall to provide a wash of soft light.

DETERMINING YOUR LIGHTING NEEDS

The first step toward improving your lighting involves careful consideration of the design and layout of your rooms and the types of activities that take place in each one.

If you're planning new lighting, you may want to draw a basic room plan (if you're building or remodeling, you can trace your architect's plans). These sketches will help you determine where to place your fixtures and where you'll want new outlets or wall switches. (See the discussion of placement on page 13.)

Lighting architectural features

You can use light both to complement the special architectural features in your house and to help disguise some aspects you'd like to downplay. As you walk through your house or go over your plans, consider the many things that light can do for you.

Room dimensions. One of the tricks light can perform is to "change" the size of a room; small rooms can become open and airy, and large rooms can be made to appear cozy and inviting.

In a small room, washing the walls with an even layer of light seems to push them outward, expanding the space. If the wall color is light, the effect is greater.

A large room illuminated with a few soft pools of light concentrated on important objects or areas becomes smaller and more intimate, as the lighted areas demand more attention than the room as a whole.

Narrow rooms benefit from trickery, too: lights along the shorter walls draw the eye away from the long ones, resulting in a "wider" space.

Ceilings can pose special problems or become special features. If your ceilings seem too low, bounced indirect light from uplights, torchères, or coves can help "raise" them. Another common problem in older homes is rough or patchy ceiling plaster. For this problem and for ceilings that seem too high, the solution is the same: keep light off the ceiling surface by using downlighting, either from surface-mounted (not recessed) fixtures or pendant fixtures. The darker surface will seem lower, and imperfections will go unnoticed.

Cathedral or beamed ceilings can take on new importance with uplighting from coves or well-placed spotlights. Many designers are using beams to hold track lighting, taking advantage of architectural lines to disguise the lengths of track.

Skylights with fixtures concealed behind diffusing panels, like the one shown on page 43, can give a feeling of continuing daylight, instead of becoming dark holes at night.

Solar rooms with a large bank of windows on the south or west side require some artificial light during certain times of day to counteract the contrast between the brightness of the sunlight and the shadows the sun produces.

Windows, sources of daylight, can pose problems at night, when they seem like dark mirrors or black holes if left uncovered. Bright diffusing lamps or fixtures can produce annoying glare and reflection in the glass. One way to avoid reflections is to light the area outside the window to a high enough level that inside lights balance with those on the outside. This use of outdoor lighting also gives the effect of extending your living area, as shown on page 17. Another solution is to use opaque pendant or can fixtures or recessed downlights, so that only the lighted areas can be seen, and not the light sources.

Window seats with small built-in downlights or wall fixtures can become cozy corners at night.

Alcoves or niches lighted with a warm glow can become focal points at night, for display or for simple variation in design.

Masonry surfaces such as brick walls or a stone fireplace take on new beauty and importance when lighted at an angle to play up their textures.

Decorative features to consider

As you think through your home's lighting, you'll want to consider several aspects of each room's decor. Basic design features such as color, the placement of furniture, and the display of decorative art can make a difference in the placement, quality, and quantity of light you'll need. How the use of color—both on room surfaces and on objects within the room—pertains to lighting is covered under "Reflectance: The key to general light levels" (at right) and "Color rendition" (page 6).

Furniture placement dictates certain lighting needs. You'll want to include at least the largest furniture pieces in your lighting plan for a given area. Consider the use of each piece. You may want wall fixtures above your buffet for serving and for ambient light. A free-standing wardrobe can be illuminated by a downlight for easier clothing selection. Bookcases and cabinets, movable or built-in, can benefit from special lighting that will help people identify the objects inside.

Artwork or collections can be lighted and displayed in a variety of ways. For some ideas on lighting artwork, see the special feature on pages 30–31. Shelf and cabinet lighting ideas are shown on pages 54–55. The light used to highlight your art or collection may also serve to augment the central downlight over your dining room table, or provide ambient light for entertaining.

Reflectance: The key to general light levels

How the color and texture of the walls, ceiling, and floors of a room contribute to the general light level depends on their reflectance—that is, the degree to which they reflect the light shed on them by windows and fixtures. The color and texture of the objects within a room also affect the overall light level.

Colors containing a lot of white reflect a larger amount of light, of course, and darker colors absorb light. A white object reflects 80 percent of the light that strikes it, while a black object reflects only 10 percent or less. For this reason, if you were to redecorate your living room by covering creamy white walls with a rich blue wallpaper, you'd soon find that you needed more light sources and higher wattage bulbs to get the same light level. The illumination in a room with light colored walls is distributed farther and more evenly as the light is reflected from surface to surface until it gradually diminishes.

Texture plays a less important role in reflectance than color does. Matte finishes diffuse light; smooth, glossy finishes bounce light directly away, reflecting it onto other surfaces. Thus a room with fabric-covered walls will require more or brighter light than a room with painted walls if it's to achieve the same light level.

Color rendition

The color of an object as we perceive it is determined by two things: the surface color of the object, and the color contained in the light shining on it. The color of a blue vase under a blue light will be heightened as the color of the light intensifies the color of the vase. Under a red light, the same blue vase will appear dull and grayish, because the red light waves are absorbed, and there are no blue waves to be reflected by the vase. This interaction between an object and a light source is called "color rendition."

Light sources give off varying amounts of color. *Daylight* or *sunlight* appears white, but actually contains the full spectrum of colors. *Incandescent light* includes colors from most of the spectrum, but has a large proportion of yellow and red. When dimmed, incandescent light becomes even more orange and red. *Fluorescent light* is generally thought to be low in red and high in green and blue light waves, but in fact there are more than 200 "colors" of fluorescent tubes available. Some of the new colored fluorescent tubes are even called "full-spectrum" and come extremely close to daylight in color.

The chart below shows how the color values of the various types of bulbs affect the apparent colors of lighted objects. Use the chart to help coordinate the colors of your lighting with your decor. If your breakfast nook is decorated in orange and yellow, for example, a warm white deluxe fluorescent will perk up your color scheme; blues will appear duller and less vivid under the same light. By the same token, of course, because light sources can alter the apparent color of fabrics and wallpaper, it's always advisable to choose furnishings and decorating materials under the same type of light you'll be using in your home.

Lighting for active living

Along with architectural and interior design factors, the activities that take place in each living area play an important part in determining your lighting needs.

Single-use areas. In working on your lighting plan, you'll find that some areas—including hallways, stairs, entries, closets, laundry areas, and workshops—host only one type of activity. These areas are the simplest to plan for; often one level of light and one set of fixtures will be sufficient.

Multiple-use areas. Family rooms, living rooms, and combination kitchen-dining rooms will prove more of a challenge. Today's family room may be the site of such diverse activities as television viewing, entertaining, piano playing, sewing, reading, and model making. The light levels required for these activities range from very soft ambient light to strong directional task lighting. And just as all of these activities aren't likely to be going on at the same time, you probably won't wish to have all the room's specialized lights on at once. What will be needed is a variety of light levels, sources, and controls.

To begin, look at the areas in your multiple-use rooms where the more exacting visual tasks are undertaken. If your family enjoys model making or working on puzzles at a table that doubles as a snacking area when you're entertaining, you might want a pendant lamp with a strong light controlled by a dimmer; the high wattage can be used whenever puzzles or models are in progress, and the dimmer used during entertaining. An adjustable floor lamp or short track system above the piano might light both sheet music and the surrounding area when your piano student is at work. For reading or sewing, a table or floor lamp with a three-way bulb next to an easy chair can be used.

Once you've provided for adequate light in task areas, you should plan for some general light to soften the contrast between task lights and surrounding areas (see "General light levels," page 9). This type of general or ambient light can come from valances over curtained windows, indirect light aimed at the ceiling or walls, or one or more dimmed lamps.

How much light do you need?

Once you've looked carefully at the architectural and decorative features in your rooms, and the activities there, you can determine the amount of light needed in each location.

Comfortable light levels are a matter of individual preference. Some people who work in brightly

(Continued on page 8)

Color effects of various bulb types

Bulb type	"Color" of light	Colors brightened	Colors grayed or muted
Incandescent	Yellow white	Warm colors	Cool colors
Fluorescent			
Cool white	Bluish white	Green, yellow, blue	Red
Warm white	Pale amber	Orange, yellow, skin tones, red	Red, blue
Cool white deluxe	White	Almost all	Almost none
Warm white deluxe	White	Red, orange, yellow	Blue
High Intensity Discharge (HID)			
Deluxe warm mercury	Yellowish white	Orange, yellow, purple, green	Deep red
Metal halide	Bluish white	Orange, yellow, blue	Deep red
High-pressure sodium	Yellow orange	Yellow, orange, light green	Deep red, deep blue, ivy green
Low-pressure sodium	Yellow	Yellow	All except yellow

WAYS TO CUT YOUR ENERGY USE

In the average household, 15 to 20 percent of all electrical power consumed is used for lighting. By carefully planning new lighting or making a few changes in your present lighting habits, you can trim your energy costs.

Residential energy standards

In an effort to conserve energy, some localities are developing residential energy standards that require a certain level of lighting efficiency in new residential construction. Check your local building code for any regulations that may apply where you live.

Even if your community has no energy standards, you can still put your house on a wattage "diet" based on the figures below. These are the recommended wattages per square foot for incandescent and fluorescent lighting.

	Incandescent	Fluorescent
Living room	5 watts	2 watts
Family room	5 watts	2 watts
Kitchen	5 watts	2 watts
Bedroom	4 watts	2 watts
Laundry	4 watts	2 watts
Workshop	5 watts	2 watts
Bathroom	3 watts	1 watt
Dining room	2 watts	1 watt
Hallway	2 watts	1 watt

Planning new lighting

Here are some guidelines to follow when you're planning new lighting:
• Provide task lighting wherever it's needed for your family's visual activities. Cut down on high levels of general lighting.
• Make it easy to turn lights off; plan for switches at room entries and exits.
• Include dimmers and timers in your plans. Solid-state dimmers, by reducing the electrical current consumed, save energy; they also extend the life of bulbs, because filaments burn at lower temperatures. Set timers to turn lights off after a given time, to keep forgotten lights in garages or laundry areas from wasting current.
• Use the daylight available from skylights and windows wherever possible.

• Choose near-white colors in your decorating—because they reflect more light, fewer light sources are needed to light brightly colored rooms.
• Use fluorescent light—it's three times as efficient, and the tubes last 5 to 20 times as long as incandescent bulbs. Shadowless fluorescent light is also excellent as a worklight, and today's deluxe fluorescent tubes produce a warm glow.
• Look for fluorescent spotlights or mercury vapor lights to use as security lights outdoors; their efficiency and long life cut costs, especially when lights are left on all night.

Change your habits to save energy

Even if you're not redesigning your lighting, you can save energy—and dollars—by following the tips below.
• Be a picky bulb buyer. Examine the packaging information on bulbs; look for the ones that will give you the most lumens (light output) per watt of electricity used.
• Use only the wattage you need—if your hallway fixture has a 100-watt bulb, for example, try stepping down to a 60-watt bulb.
• Turn lights off when they're not in use—even fluorescent lights; with their improved ballasts, frequent starting won't appreciably shorten the life of today's fluorescent tubes.
• Buy reading lamps with three-way capacity for added flexibility; keep them on low when they're not needed for tasks.
• Put lower-wattage reflector bulbs in directional fixtures to focus the light where it's needed instead of trapping it in the fixtures.
• In nightlight fixtures, use clear 4-watt bulbs rather than 7-watt coated bulbs. They'll last as long, and use only half as much energy.
• Replace old, darkened bulbs; they provide less light while using the same amount of energy they did when they were new.
• Clean fixtures, globes, and bulbs regularly—dust and dirt absorb light.
• Install photocell-controlled on/off switches in outdoor fixtures so they'll stay on only at night.
• Wherever possible, use fewer bulbs. A single 100-watt bulb gives out 1750 lumens, while four 25-watt bulbs provide 940 lumens for the same amount of energy. And the 100-watt bulb costs less than the four 25-watt bulbs.

. . . Continued from page 6

lighted offices grow accustomed to this kind of environment and want the same level of light in their homes. Other people feel more relaxed and secure in relatively low light levels, preferring to illuminate primarily the area in which they're reading, working, or relaxing, while the rest of the room falls into gentle shadow.

For many years Americans have lived in relative brightness indoors—the light levels recommended by our lighting engineers have been much higher than those recommended in Europe. But with the new accent on energy conservation, our engineers are scaling down recommended levels. The trend now is toward providing bright lighting in task areas, with surroundings more softly lit, rather than trying to achieve uniform brightness.

How much light is "enough" light? Lighting designers and engineers have several technical methods of determining how much light is needed for specific tasks under specific conditions. But without being an engineer, you too can measure the amount of light available in a given room and make reliable estimates of the light levels you'll need.

Factors that affect light levels.
When you're determining how much light is needed for a given activity, weigh these factors: 1) the difficulty of the task to be performed; 2) the speed and accuracy with which it must be completed; 3) the color contrasts among the materials involved in the task; and 4) the eyesight of the person who will be engaged in the activity. If an older person will be doing embroidery on a dark cloth with richly colored thread, for example, lots of light will probably be required; the task calls for a high degree of accuracy, and the weak contrast between the fabric and thread is hard on older eyes, which are often less sharp than a younger person's. For less demanding visual activities, such as reading the newspaper or watching television, light levels can be much lower.

Measuring lumens.
One method for measuring and planning light levels involves the amount of light emitted by each bulb, which is

Lumen output of standard household bulbs and tubes

Incandescent

Watts	Lumens
25	235
40	455
60	870
75	1190
100	1750
150	2880
50/100/150	580/1670/2250

Fluorescent

Watts	Lumens
20	820
40	2150
40 (U-shaped)	1980
22 (circular)	800
40 (circular)	1900

measured in *lumens.* If you look at the sleeve around a light bulb, you'll see that it states both the bulb's wattage (the amount of electricity used by the bulb) and the number of lumens, or amount of light, that the bulb produces. Lumen outputs vary from manufacturer to manufacturer, and diminish as bulbs age. The chart above lists the average initial lumen output for a variety of standard household bulbs.

As a rule of thumb, the most difficult visual tasks—like embroidery—require a total of at least 2500 lumens in an average room, with the greatest number of lumens concentrated at the work location. A casual task, such as watching television, requires from 1500 to 2000 lumens. To find the number of lumens available in a given room, area, or lighting plan, add up the lumen outputs of all the bulbs involved.

For close, precise work, you might want a table lamp with a three-way bulb switched to high, providing 2250 lumens, immediately next to the work area, while another nearby lamp with a 60-watt bulb adds another 850 lumens. Roughly the same total of lumens could also be supplied by two 100-watt bulbs or four 60-watt bulbs, arrayed around the work area, but common sense calls for a greater concentration of light at the work area.

Measuring footcandles.
A second and more precise method of measuring light levels uses the *footcandle,* or the amount of illumination provided by one lumen distributed over a surface one foot square. As a measure of the light on a surface, footcandles are more useful than lumens as a guide to task lighting levels.

Camera light meter footcandle readings

F-Stop	Footcandles
f 2	10
f 3.5	15
f 4	20
f 4.5	30
f 5.6	40
f 6.3	60
f 8	80
f 9	120
f 11	160
f 14	240

Experts measure footcandles with a special footcandle meter, but you can use the light meter built into a 35-mm. camera. To find the footcandles of light reaching your kitchen counter, for example, place a large sheet of white paper or cardboard on the counter at a 45-degree angle. Set the camera's ASA meter at 100 and the shutter speed at $1/30$ of a

Recommended minimum footcandles

Activity	Footcandles
Entertaining	10–20
Dining	10–20
Casual reading	20–50
Grooming	20–50
Kitchen, laundry—general light	20–50
Kitchen—food preparation	50–100
Prolonged reading or studying	50–100
Workshop activities	50–100
Sewing, medium-colored fabric	50–100
Sewing, dark fabrics	100–200
Hobbies involving fine detail	100–200

second. Without throwing a shadow on the card, line up the card through the camera's viewfinder and adjust the f-stop to the proper exposure for taking a picture. The f-stop reading you get will tell you the approximate footcandle level as translated in the table at left.

Lighting designers and engineers have determined standard footcandle levels needed to perform ordinary household tasks. The chart below left includes both a high and a low number of footcandles; the high is recommended for difficult tasks or for older people; the low is for easier tasks or younger people. Here again, these are recommended levels, and you may feel comfortable with more or less light.

General light levels. Though providing enough light for task areas is of primary importance, care should also be taken to light the surrounding areas with general (ambient) light. If these areas were not at least softly lighted, whenever you looked up your eyes would have to compensate for the change between high and low light levels, resulting in eyestrain.

In rooms where you have task lighting, the recommended general light level is 20 footcandles or about a third of the footcandle value in the task area, whichever is less. For rooms where the main activities are entertaining or relaxing, 5 to 10 footcandles are recommended. Entries, stairs, halls, and other passageways should also have a general light level of 5 to 10 footcandles.

SELECTING LIGHT FIXTURES

Once you've determined the quality and quantity of light you need, you're ready for a visit to the local lighting, hardware, or electrical supply store—or are you?

Put off that trip for a bit, and make it a point to observe the lighting in your favorite restaurant, your bank, a boutique, or a neighbor's house. Look for "living" examples of all the types of lighting

presented in this book, and sort out those you prefer from those you don't like. Then, with your needs and preferences in mind, you'll be ready to hunt for the fixtures that provide exactly the type of lighting you want.

Factors to weigh in selecting fixtures

If you've formed some ideas about the kinds of lighting you need, selecting fixtures would appear to be easy. But given the great variety available today, finding the right fixtures can be confusing and complicated. Here's some help:

Function. All types of lighting systems include fixtures that give strong directional light, general diffused light, or a combination, as shown in the illustrations below.

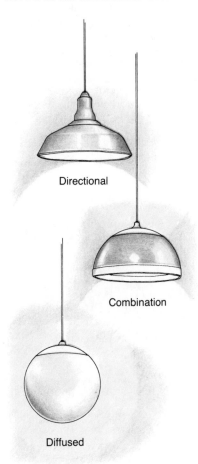

Directional

Combination

Diffused

One of the primary considerations about any fixture is how it directs the light. Will it put the light you want where you want it?

Make sure that directional fixtures have a high enough maximum bulb wattage to allow you to use bulbs strong enough to "throw" the light from the fixtures to task or display areas.

Size. Fixtures on display will often look smaller in the store than they will in your home. Take measurements of your top choices; then find bowls or boxes of the appropriate sizes at home, and hold them in place to determine if the fixtures you have in mind are the proper scale. Manufacturers often produce standard fixtures in graded sizes, so be sure to ask suppliers about other sizes.

Design. Here, personal taste will be your guide, leading you to whatever suits your decor. Designers and architects have found that a sense of decorative continuity can be created by the use of similar fixtures throughout a home. Responding to this, manufacturers offer "families" of fixtures available as spotlights, pendants, track lights, and ceiling fixtures.

Flexibility. Because our tastes and habits often change, flexibility is an important consideration when choosing fixtures. If you change your display of artwork, you'll want to adjust your lighting, too. Movable or adjustable lamps are a longtime favorite partly because they're so flexible. With track systems, you can alter the location of fixtures along the track as well as the way each fixture is aimed. Even some built-in recessed downlights have changeable trim, so that a regular downlight can become a pinhole light or an eyeball.

Cost. You'll want to consider both purchase price and operating costs in selecting lighting fixtures. When a fixture is to be kept burning for several hours at a stretch, it may be wise to invest in a more costly low-energy unit than to buy a less expensive kilowatt-eater. More expensive fixtures are likely to offer more flexibility and higher engineering quality, producing more controlled light; you may want to use these in your living room or wherever such quality is important.

Maintenance. To operate efficiently, all fixtures should be cleaned regularly. So keep in mind that kitchens, bathrooms, and work areas demand fixtures that are easy to clean. Since all light bulbs must be changed eventually, consider using a simple fixture with a long-lived fluorescent bulb for the top of the stairs and other hard-to-reach spots.

TYPES OF FIXTURES

To help distinguish the ways that each type can be used, fixtures are categorized in the following sections according to how they're installed. Within each category you'll find fixtures that will provide the quality of light you need.

Movable light fixtures

Table lamps, floor lamps, and small specialty lamps are easy to buy, easy to change, and easy to take along when you move.

Table lamps, as decorative tools, show individuality and style while serving as sources of light. Variety, mobility, and ease of installation add to the appeal of table lamps.

(On pages 68–69 you'll find ideas for lamps you can create.)

The choice of a lampshade can be crucial to the effectiveness of a table lamp. As illustrated below left, a difference of 2 inches in the diameter of the lower edge of the shade can make a significant difference in the spread of light shed by a lamp.

The height of the bulb within the shade also affects the circle of light. As shown below, light will spread farther when the bulb is set low in the shade. Small extension screws used on the lamp harp to adjust the height of the shade are available at most lighting supply stores.

Floor lamps offer great flexibility. One type—the *traditional floor lamp* with a large central bulb and three smaller ones—provides a combination of levels, serving either as a reading light or as a source of soft ambient light. Bright *torchères* bounce light onto the ceiling for a dramatic form of indirect illumination. Unobtrusive *pharmacy lamps* offer new options, too, especially for tasks such as reading and sewing. Lamps with adjustable directional fixtures—such as *three-source* floor or pole lamps—are a practical choice for task lighting.

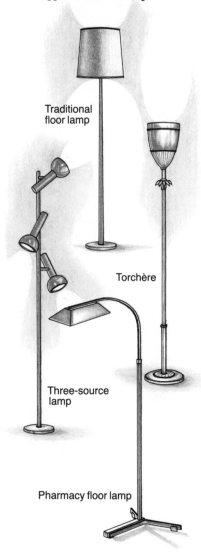

Types of floor lamps

Traditional floor lamp

Torchère

Three-source lamp

Pharmacy floor lamp

Specialty lamps in new varieties are appearing on the market. These new lamps, like the traditional picture light and drafting table lamp, can fill a definite need while remaining movable, and they require no special wiring. Easily adjusted *clip-on lights* are practical for providing task lighting over beds, desks, and shelves. *Uplight cans* highlight indoor plants or wash walls with light for instant decorating touches. *Mini-reflector spotlights* are handy for pinpointing paintings or sculpture from a nearby mantelpiece or shelf. *High intensity lamps*, often adjustable, supply a small bright spot of light while taking up little space.

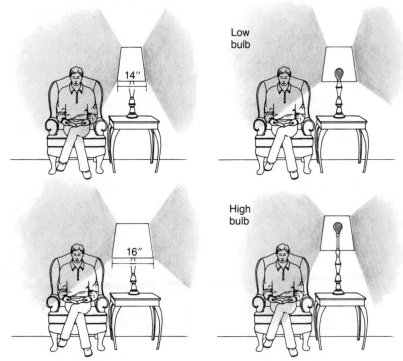

Low bulb

High bulb

Light spread results from shade diameter (left) and bulb height (right).

Types of specialty lamps

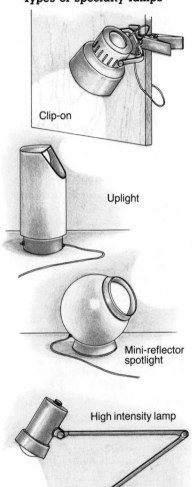

Clip-on

Uplight

Mini-reflector
spotlight

High intensity lamp

Surface-mounted fixtures

Installed either on walls or on ceilings, surface-mounted fixtures are integral to most home lighting designs. Generally, surface-mounted fixtures can be added without a great deal of wiring work.

Track lighting offers great versatility and ease of installation. Available in varying lengths, tracks are really extended electrical lines from the outlets they plug into; fixtures can be mounted anywhere along each line.

A track can be flush-mounted or suspended, and used on ceilings or walls, often without the addition of extra wiring. Track fixtures should generally be close to the wall they're meant to light—

within 2 to 4 feet. For safety, avoid track lighting in wet areas such as bathrooms.

Tracks come in one and two-circuit varieties; the two-circuit type gives you the flexibility of having two sets of lights operating independently.

Tracks can accommodate hanging lamps, fluorescent tubes, and special low-voltage spotlights, in addition to theatrical, high-tech, and traditional-style fixtures (see drawing below).

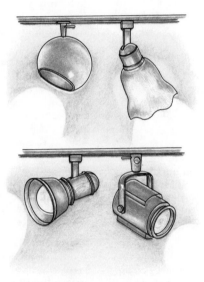

Four track lights show style range.

Chandeliers and pendant fixtures

add sparkle and style in high-ceilinged entries and above dining and game tables. These decorative fixtures can give direct or diffused light—or a combination of the two—for different purposes, as shown in the drawing on page 9.

The proportion of the fixture in relation to its surroundings is critical—if used over a table, the width of the fixture should be at least 12 inches less than the width of the table to prevent collisions with diners or passers-by. Hanging it about 30 inches above the table surface helps avoid glare. In an entry, be sure to allow enough room below the chandelier to guarantee safe passage for tall people.

Some pendant fixtures, such as the popular fan-plus-light combination, are quite heavy. To install them, follow the directions for heavy surface-mounted fixtures on page 87.

Ceiling and wall fixtures provide general illumination in traffic areas such as landings, entries, and hallways, where safety is a consideration. Kitchens, baths, and workshops benefit from the added light from ceiling fixtures used in conjunction with task lighting on work surfaces.

Fixtures in this category range from functional frosted glass globes to delicate candlelike sconces. When selecting a fixture, look closely at the amount of light that bounces off the wall or ceiling to be sure the light will be directed where you want it. Don't overlook the possibilities of a single adjustable fixture that you can redirect when you rearrange furniture.

Recessed ceiling fixtures

Recessed downlights offer light without the intrusion of a visible fixture. For this reason, they're effective in rooms with low ceilings and sleek lines. Basically a dome with a light bulb set in the top, a recessed downlight can be fitted with any one of a number of trims that aim the light to fit the function desired.

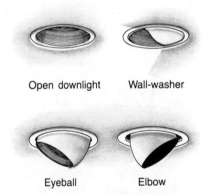

Open downlight   Wall-washer

Eyeball   Elbow

Trims modify recessed ceiling lights.

When used over sinks and countertops in kitchens, an *open downlight* with a glare-cutting baffle spreads a strong task light over the work surfaces. Open fixtures are also good for lighting stairs and entries.

Equipped as a *wall-washer* fixture, a recessed downlight throws light onto a nearby wall; a series of such fixtures can be used for even, balanced lighting of a wall of artwork or bookcases. Nor-

(Continued on page 13)

FOR A SAFE AND SECURE HOUSE

Well-planned lighting can make your house safer. Master switches and remote controls let you turn on interior lights from another room or from outside the house. Timers and daylight-sensitive photocells make it appear that someone's home when the house is empty. With motion-sensitive, sound-sensitive, and touch controls, lights blaze as soon as someone enters a room, makes a noise, steps on a rug, or touches a metallic object.

In placing outdoor lights, you should take into account both security and esthetic factors. See pages 78–79 for more information about outdoor lighting.

Look in the Yellow Pages under "Electric Supplies—Retail," "Lighting Fixtures," or "Electronic Equipment & Supplies—Dealers" for the equipment you'll need.

Master switches. Master switches can be used to operate lights in various rooms both inside the house and outdoors. Two types of master switch consoles are available: plug-ins, which control plug-in light fixtures; and wire-ins, which control wired-in lights. If you want to use a plug-in console for outdoor lights, a receiving station must be wired into the outdoor lighting circuit.

Remote controls. The same size as units used to open garage doors, and operated on the same principle, these battery-powered, hand-held transmitters send out radio waves. A receiving station wired into one or two circuits of your home near the circuit distribution center turns interior or exterior lights on or off. Because the system also operates on a special wall-mounted switch, you can leave the transmitter in your car. Receiving station and wall switch wiring is best left to an electrician.

Timers. These devices are constructed in two ways. A solid-state timer has no moving parts to make noise or wear out, and is far more accurate than its motor-drive cousin. It costs more, though, and controls only incandescent lights. A motor-driven timer controls both incandescent and fluorescent lights.

Some solid-state and motor-driven timers can be programmed in 24-hour cycles, others in 7-day cycles. A 7-day timer lets you vary the times the lights will go on and off each night within a period of 7 days.

Daylight-sensitive photocells. A photocell that "monitors" the daylight closes a circuit when the sun goes down, turning on outdoor or indoor lights. When dawn comes, the cells break open the circuit, shutting off the lights. A timer can be wired into the circuit; an override switch lets you operate the lights manually.

Though momentary bursts of light such as lightning or passing headlights have no effect on the operation of a photocell, it must be mounted so that artificial light won't strike it continuously for longer than 90 seconds.

Motion-sensitive controls. Like magic, the lights go on as soon as someone enters a room: motion-sensitive controls are triggered by an object's breaking through an infrared beam or into a field of ultrasonic waves. The lights go out again when no motion occurs within a manually adjusted, preset time (a range of 1 to 12 minutes is typical). Ultrasonic sensors that produce the fewest number of waves are the least expensive; but they can often be heard by dogs and sometimes by humans, so an in-home trial is a good idea before you buy one of these models. Installation of a motion sensor is a job for an electrician.

Sound-sensitive controls. The light-switching sensor in these microcomputers can be adjusted to any level of audible sound. When no sound occurs within the time you set on the switch (7 seconds to 7 minutes is typical), the lights go out—unless you use the overriding manual switch to keep the lights on for quiet activities like reading.

Many sound-sensitive devices wire into an ordinary wall switch box, much as wall-mounted dimmers do (see page 86); some units even contain their own dimmers.

Touch controls. One type of touch—or rather step—control is a mat that slides under a rug. It's laced with pressure-sensitive wires; any pressure turns the lights on or off. Unless you can find a plug-in unit containing its own transformer, it's best to have an electrician do the installation.

With the other type of touch control, you can get any of three levels of illumination by touching any metallic part of a light fixture. The control device itself screws into an ordinary lamp socket; you then screw an incandescent bulb into the touch control. You can also run #18 TW wire from the control to a nongrounded metal object, such as a metal planter or window frame, turning that object into a touch-sensitive light control.

. . . Continued from page 11

mally, wall-washing fixtures are mounted in a series 3 feet from the wall to be washed, with 3 feet between fixtures. An adjustable *eyeball* or *elbow* fixture highlights objects on a wall.

Recessed fixtures can be added in existing ceilings, provided there's enough space between the ceiling and the floor above. These fixtures range from $5^1/4$ inches to more than 12 inches in depth, though some manufacturers offer shallower fixtures for use in tight spaces.

Because glare can be a problem with downlighting, reflective interior finishes, baffles, lenses, and louvers (similar to those shown below right) have been developed to direct the light away

Types of built-in indirect lighting

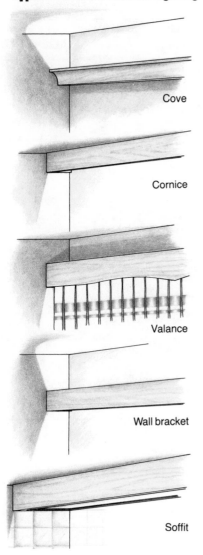

Cove

Cornice

Valance

Wall bracket

Soffit

from people's sightlines. In general, fixtures with deeply inset bulbs will produce less glare.

Built-in indirect lighting

Coves, cornices, valances, wall brackets, and soffits can be used when indirect lighting is desired. Simple and architectural in design, these devices ensure that light sources are shielded from view, allowing light to spill out around the shields (see drawing below left).

Coves direct light upward onto the ceiling, while *cornices* spread light below. Used over windows, *valances* send light both up to the ceiling and down over draperies. *Wall brackets*, mounted directly onto interior walls, spread light both up and down, and can be used to highlight artwork or to provide ambient light in living areas. *Soffits*, used over work areas, throw a stronger light directly below.

Luminous ceilings, used most often in kitchens and work areas, provide an even wash of light throughout a room.

PLACEMENT CONSIDERATIONS

Though seemingly unimportant, the careful placement of switches, outlets, and fixtures can be essential in a successful lighting scheme.

Switches and outlets

Using the room plans you've drawn, you can designate the location of switches and outlets by using the symbols given on page 83. Draw these on your own plans or look for them on your architect's plans. For safety and security, be sure you can control at least one outlet or fixture at the entry to each room. Draw a line from the switch to designate which light it serves. Check to see that the same light can be turned off at the opposite exit of the room—or at your bedside, if you're dealing with bedroom lighting. Provide an outlet on the wall near tables or desks where you'll want to plug in

lamps, clocks, or appliances. It's better to provide extra outlets than to have too few and need a tangle of extension cords. Instructions for adding outlets or switches in your present rooms begin on page 88.

Fixtures

Several things will influence the placement of your light fixtures. With their fixtures, manufacturers often provide specific placement instructions according to room dimensions, the type of lighting effect you want, and the beam spread or cone of light produced by individual fixtures and bulbs.

One of the most important considerations in the placement of light fixtures is the glare produced by bulbs. When considering use of such fixtures in areas where people will be sitting, be sure the light will not be so bright as to disturb anyone's line of vision. Deeply recessed fixtures or fixtures with good baffles or pinhole apertures will help solve the problem of glare. The finish of the reflector (interior surface) of the fixture can also affect the amount of glare; choose the finish that provides the brightness level you desire. Clip-on louvers and shutters, like those shown below, help cut glare.

Devices to control glare

Reflector finish

Color filter

Honeycomb louver

Ring louver

Snoot extension

Barn door shutter

LIGHT BULBS AND TUBES

Light bulbs and tubes can be grouped in general categories according to the way they produce light.

Incandescent light, the kind used most often in our homes, is produced by a tungsten thread that burns slowly inside a glass bulb.

Low-voltage incandescent lighting for indoor use is new on the residential scene. Operating on 12 or 24 volts, these lights require transformers (which are often built into the fixtures) to step down the voltage from standard 120-volt household circuits. The small bulbs are useful in accent lighting, where light must be projected and precisely directed onto a small area. Low-voltage track and ceiling fixtures are relatively expensive to buy; but in general, low-voltage lighting can be energy-efficient if carefully planned.

Fluorescent light is produced when electrical energy and mercury vapor create an arc that stimulates the phosphors coating the inside of the bulb. Because the light comes evenly from the whole surface of the tube, it spreads in all directions, creating a steady, shadowless light. Fluorescent tubes require a ballast to ignite and maintain the electrical flow.

High intensity discharge (HID) bulbs produce light when electricity excites specific gases in pressurized bulbs. Requiring special fixtures and ballasts, these lights may take up to 7 minutes to ignite after being switched on. The color emitted by HID bulbs is rather unflattering, but they offer long life and high efficiency.

Neon light is also generated when electricity passes through a gas: neon gas, for example, glows orange red, and other gases give off a variety of colors. Neon tubes' low light output makes them undesirable as a functional light source. Requiring a 24-volt transformer, neon fixtures can be expensive to buy, though they don't use much energy and may last for years.

		Type
Incandescent		A-bulb
		Three-way
		Long-life
		G—Globe
		T—Tubular
		Decorative
		R—Reflector
		PAR—Parabolic aluminized reflector
		ER—Ellipsoidal reflector
		Silvered bowl
		Tungsten-halogen
Low-voltage incandescent		Low-voltage reflector spot
		Low-voltage PAR
		Low-voltage mini-reflector
		Low-voltage mini-lights
Fluorescent		Tube
		U-shaped
		Circle
High intensity discharge (HID)		Mercury vapor
		Metal halide
		High-pressure sodium
		Low-pressure sodium

Description	Uses	Efficiency (lumens per watt)	Bulb life in hours	Watts
Familiar pear shape; frosted and clear.	Everyday household use.	12 to 21	750 to 1,000	4 to 300
A-bulb shape; frosted. Two filaments provide three light levels.	In lamps with special switches in multiuse areas.	11 to 15	1,000 to 1,600	30/70/100 to 100/200/300
A-bulb shape; frosted. Burns slowly at lower light output.	In hard-to-reach fixtures.	12 to 17	1,150 to 3,000	40 to 150
Ball-shaped bulb, 2" to 6" in diameter. Frosted or clear.	Often decorative; without shades or in pendant fixtures.	12 to 21	1,500 to 4,000	15 to 100
Tube-shaped, from 5" long. Frosted or clear.	Appliances, cabinets, decorative fixtures.	7.5 to 10	1,000	15 to 60
Flame-shaped; specially coated.	In chandeliers and sconces.	—	1,500 to 4,000	15 to 60
White or silvered coating directs light out end of funnel-shaped bulb.	In directional fixtures; focuses light where needed.	7 to 12.2	1,500 to 4,000	25 to 300
Similar to auto headlamp; special shape and coating project light and control beam.	In recessed downlights and track fixtures.	8 to 13	2,000 to 6,000	25 to 250
Shape and coating focus light 2" ahead of bulb, then light spreads out.	Can replace higher-wattage bulbs in recessed downlights.	11.3 to 12.3	1,500 to 4,000	50 to 120
A-bulb in shape, with silvered cap to cut glare and produce indirect light.	Can be used in track fixtures and recessed downlights.	—	1,000	60 to 200
Small tube-shaped bulb with consistently high light output; used in special fixtures.	Small fixtures with reflectors for reading or indirect light.	18 to 22	2,000	100 to 500
Similar to standard R-bulb; directs light in various beam spreads and distances.	In low-voltage track fixtures and recessed downlights.	—	500 to 2,000	15, 25
Similar to auto headlight; tiny filament, shape, and coating give precise direction.	To project a small spot of light a long distance.	—	2,000	25, 50
Tiny (2" diameter) projector bulb; gives small circle of light from a distance.	In low-voltage track fixtures and recessed downlights.	—	500 to 5,000	25, 50
Like Christmas tree lights; encased in flexible, waterproof plastic.	Decorative, to add sparkle.	—	22 years (est.)	0.84
Tube-shaped, 5" to 40" long. Needs special fixture and ballast.	Shadowless work light; also indirect lighting.	48 to 90	6,000 to 20,000	8 to 40
U-shaped for greater localized light output; 18" to 24" long.	Some small U-tubes include ballasts to replace A-bulbs.	48 to 70	7,500 to 12,000	27 to 40
6" to 12" circle; some types require special fixtures, others can replace A-bulbs.	In compact circle fixtures.	48 to 70	12,000	20 to 40
Bulb-within-a-bulb, shaped like an oversized A-bulb; needs special ballast.	Available as garden and security lighting for residential use.	63	16,000 to 24,000	50 to 1,000
Similar to mercury vapor, almost twice as efficient; needs special ballast and fixture.	Outdoor security lighting. Now available in table lamp wattages with self-ballast.	115	10,000 to 20,000	175 to 1,500
Similar to mercury vapor. Gold-hued light. Needs special ballast and fixture.	Outdoor lighting; used indoors commercially and industrially.	140	10,000 to 24,000	35 to 1,000
U-shaped tube within larger bulb. Most efficient light source. Needs ballast and fixture.	Street, highway, and security lighting.	183	10,000 to 18,000	18 to 180

ROOM-BY-ROOM LIGHTING INSPIRATION

G E N E R A L • T A S K • A C C E N T

Here is the idea section of this book, designed to get your creativity flowing. It includes "enlightening" examples for every room of the house, from the entry to the basement workshop, covering a variety of design situations and lighting techniques.

Take a careful look

Though light is elusive, and its effects difficult to capture in photographs, spend a few minutes with the photos here that interest you. Look closely, and you'll discover a great deal.

The majority of the photos were taken at night, with a minimum of photographer's lights, in an effort to let the lighting in each picture stand on its own. This should make it easier for you to judge what kind of light is actually present, and exactly how it affects the environment. In some cases, the fixtures will be evident; in others, you'll see only the lighted surfaces. Try to look beyond the decor in each photo and consider the light itself, to see if it's playing tricks or if it's straightforward and simple.

Artist's sketches of some of the installations featured—where details weren't immediately evident in the photographs—have been included, in case you'd like to adapt the same type of lighting to fit your needs. A number of these

drawings include measurements, primarily to provide a sense of scale—your applications will probably call for a different set of specifications. The wiring know-how necessary for installing most of the examples shown can be found in the wiring section at the end of this book (pages 80–95).

Putting ideas into action

Whether you're building or remodeling, or just want to see your house in a new light, you'll find guidance in the following pages.

For special problems—lighting artwork, plants, shelves, and cabinets—you'll find two special features full of suggestions on pages 30–31 and 50–51.

To try out your lighting ideas, see the instructions for making a basic lighting kit on pages 40–41. With this easy-to-assemble kit, you can experiment with different types of light in your own home without first investing in expensive fixtures.

If you'd like to try your own ingenuity, take a look at the basic instructions for making lamps from everyday materials on pages 68–69—and don't be afraid to create your own variations.

What to do outdoors? You'll find pointers on lighting the outside of your home and yard, with an eye to both decorative and security lighting, on pages 78–79.

Where to go for more help

In reading the captions for the photographs that follow, you may notice that the lighting designs featured were planned by a cross section of consultants that includes lighting designers, architects, interior designers, and knowledgeable homeowners. In some cases, two or more such people collaborated on a project, for a balance of effective lighting and decorative treatment.

When looking for help, keep in mind what kind of expertise you can expect from each type of professional. Lighting designers will calculate the light levels and beams needed in a given space, and then determine the fixtures and placement required. Architects often choose to highlight the special architectural features of a building while providing light for functional purposes. Interior designers, concentrating on total decor, will often choose fixtures for their decorative as well as functional value. If you're aware of these professional tendencies, as well as your own preferences, you can choose the type of professional with whom you'll work best. In any case, let your own style and needs be your guide in planning your lighting.

For additional information, refer to "The Basics of Good Lighting" on pages 4–15.

Accent on architectural lighting

Sparkling low-voltage mini-lights focus attention on the
striking high windows in this easy but elegant living
room. A concealed fluorescent fixture highlights the niche
above the mantel; the candles add a warm, festive tone.
Sleek brass lamps behind each sofa provide reading
light where and when it's needed. Floodlights on the
plantings outside seem to extend the boundaries of the
room, while their brightness eliminates reflections on
the glass inside. Architects: MLTW Turnbull Associates.
Lighting design: Richard Peters.

ENTRIES / A bright welcome to the house

Entries should be warmly lighted, enticing guests to come further inside. Effective fixtures range from the eye-catching and exciting to the simple and functional. They can set the house's lighting style.

Because entries often join hallways or stairs, give careful consideration to lighting for safety. Wall or ceiling fixtures can be placed to guide guests into the traffic pattern.

A light for the coat closet and one near a mirror for that last-minute check make entry lighting complete.

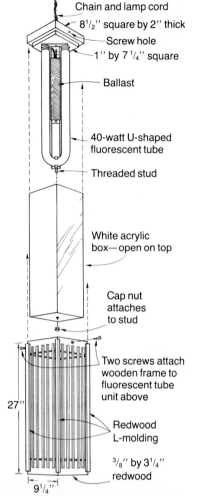

Chain and lamp cord
8¹/₂'' square by 2'' thick
Screw hole
1'' by 7¹/₄'' square
Ballast
40-watt U-shaped fluorescent tube
Threaded stud
White acrylic box—open on top
Cap nut attaches to stud
Two screws attach wooden frame to fluorescent tube unit above
27''
Redwood L-molding
³/₈'' by 3¹/₄'' redwood
9¹/₄''

Light on three levels

Suspended from the two-story-high ceiling, these redwood-trimmed rectangular lanterns light the balcony passage above as well as the entry below. Constructed by the home-owner according to the drawing at right, the wood trim and acrylic diffusing boxes warm the light emitted by the U-shaped fluorescent tubes within. Architect: Kenneth Lim.

Aglow from above

A sunlit welcome during the day becomes a glowing nighttime greeting, as light shines from the four pairs of frosted globe bulbs that frame this skylight. The globes fill the skylight and the area below with a gentle radiance. Architect: Kenneth J. Abler.

Lines of light lead you inside

Guiding visitors into the house, these semirecessed
fluorescent fixtures are fitted with reflectors and disk
baffles that direct the light upward, where it bounces
off the walls and ceiling for an airy, open feeling.
Architects: MLTW Turnbull Associates. Lighting design:
Richard Peters.

Providing light for an active family's needs in living rooms and family rooms can be a challenge. You'll want to include *task* lighting for reading, games, or handiwork, as well as *accent* lighting on artwork or architectural features. Low levels of *ambient* (general) light set a congenial mood for entertaining or watching television.

Dimmers and three-way bulbs in lamps make fixtures do double duty—the highest level serves as task light, and the lowest provides ambient light.

Lights focused on artwork or bookshelves provide both ambient light and a type of accent lighting. Valances, cornices, and baffles are effective ambient sources, too.

Making the most of accent lighting

Main sources of this room's light are the wall-washer fixture aimed at the print over the mantel, and the track spotlights over the sideboard. A small recessed fixture brightens the window seat. Architect: Michael D. Moyer. Interior design: Barbara Wolfe Interiors.

Corner combination of lamplight and spotlights

This cozy corner lends itself to reading, playing games, or snacking. Wide-shaded lamp spreads a broad circle of light for people who want to work while sitting on the couch, which was made from an antique iron bed. Swiveling spotlights, fitted with 50-watt reflector bulbs, are handsome and functional replacements for an old standard ceiling fixture. Interior design: Jean Chappell.

Twin lamps lend their light

A "popped-out" window brightens this room by catching daylight on three sides. At night, the window area is illuminated by two hand-crafted lamps sitting on a ledge behind the couch. The lamp bases, made from a pair of etched clay pots, were finished with rounds of clear pine (see drawing below). Pots and pine were then treated with a sealant for a low-gloss finish.

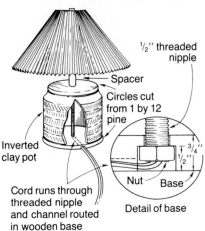

1/2" threaded nipple

Spacer

Circles cut from 1 by 12 pine

Inverted clay pot

Cord runs through threaded nipple and channel routed in wooden base

Nut   Base

3/4"   1/2"

Detail of base

. . . LIVING AREAS

Color and light dramatize the decor

Vases, pillows, and bowls throughout this cream-toned room seem to vibrate with color, thanks to illumination with colored light that strengthens their own hues. In addition to low-voltage track fixtures, which supply accent lighting, an uplight under the plant creates giant shadows and the brass reading lamp provides task lighting. On the floor, a glowing globe adds interest. Half-bowl wall fixtures in the window corners send light up to the ceiling, and a splash of red from a track fixture floats above the city lights beyond. Lighting design: Randall Whitehead. Interior design: Christian Wright.

Subtle light source

Simple in design, this display pedestal gently illuminates the statue of Saint Francis, accenting its graceful lines and creating a halo of light on the wall behind it. The box was made of pressboard, covered with fabric, and topped with acrylic, as the illustration below shows. Three vent holes in the rear allow heat from the bulb to escape. Design: Marc Miyasato.

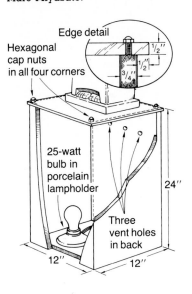

Edge detail

Hexagonal cap nuts in all four corners

1/2"
1/2"
3/4"

25-watt bulb in porcelain lampholder

24"

Three vent holes in back

12"   12"

Neon—a novel notion

A simple rectangle of white neon is used both to accent the architectural lines of this niche and to light it when it serves as a display stage. Tracks for glass shelves have been built in along either side to accommodate another type of display. Architect: Ted Tanaka.

Striking set of overlapping rectangles

A suspended chrome track system interacts with the ceiling beams above and the squared seating unit below to add architectural interest. With the track system wired on two circuits, the fixtures aimed in on the conversation area can be dimmed independently from those aimed outward as accent lights. Louvers have been installed over lights that might shine in guests' eyes. A matching uplight fixture creates dappled shadows of the *Ficus benjamina*. Design: Pennington and Pennington.

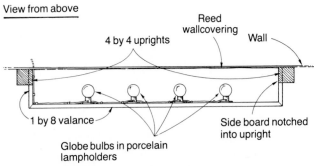

View from above

Reed wallcovering

Wall

4 by 4 uprights

1 by 8 valance

Side board notched into upright

Globe bulbs in porcelain lampholders

Built-in bench lighting

This informal bench is lighted from above by its own wall bracket. The ambient light spreads down over the reed paper and artwork and up to the ceiling. Four small porcelain lampholders, wired in series, are fastened to the face board and connected to a nearby wall switch (see drawing above). Design: Stanford Electric Works.

A study in understatement

A soft glow of indirect lighting complements the muted tones and textures of furnishings in this corner sitting area. Built in behind the seating unit as shown in the drawing below, fluorescent fixtures bathe the area in a particularly subtle kind of light. Interior design: Nancy Glenn.

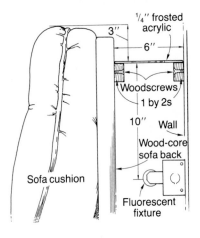

1/4" frosted acrylic

3"

6"

Woodscrews

1 by 2s

10"   Wall

Wood-core sofa back

Sofa cushion

Fluorescent fixture

**For special effect:
Antique Chinese jar
made into a modern lamp**

This table lamp holds a position of
importance in the room at right, adding a dash of bright color as well as
light. The lamp was professionally
made from an antique porcelain jar;
a dark wooden cap and base were
added as finishing touches. Design:
Ruth Soforenko.

Downplayed fixtures set the scene

Open, recessed downlights on dimmers create versatile
general lighting in this room, where the fixtures themselves go virtually unnoticed. The overhang above the
fireplace hides a short segment of track, which holds a
spotlight for each painting. The jar lamp adds a well-
placed task light, while a spotlight above it accents the
plant. Behind the oriental screen in the background is
another downlight, generating a soft, ambient glow.
Interior design: Ruth Soforenko.

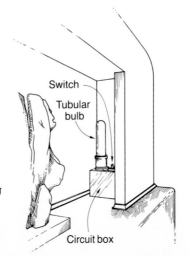

Fireplace focal point

The addition of a light in the niche above this fireplace gives depth and focus to a subtle layering of structural curves and arches. The echoing curves of the smoky coral piece are dramatized by the sidelighting provided by a simple tubular bulb (see drawing at right). Architect: Pamela M. Seifert.

Switch

Tubular bulb

Circuit box

Art lighting illuminates room

Spanning the width of the room, this enameled cylinder houses a series of fluorescent tubes. A special reflector, shown in the detail below, directs the light onto the white wall—which, in turn, reflects a gentle light throughout the room. The ringed baffle cuts glare and lends a rosy tint to the light. Architects: MLTW Turnbull Associates. Lighting design: Richard Peters.

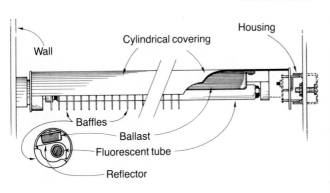

Wall

Cylindrical covering

Housing

Baffles

Ballast

Fluorescent tube

Reflector

For family living

In a country setting, this addition designed for a family with growing children combines a kitchen, eating area, and family space in one large, open room. Four deeply recessed ceiling fixtures light the family space. Dimmers that control the 150-watt floodlights can be used to gear the light to comfortable levels, from bright to dim, depending on the family's activities and mood. Architect: Jack Woodson. Lighting design: James Cooper. Interior design: Design Professionals Incorporated.

Wet-bar brightener

Ready for entertaining, this perky family room wet bar includes a built-in downlight to make serving easier. If the light's left on with the shutters closed, it provides an interesting ambient light as it peeps through the shutter cracks. Interior design: Ruth Soforenko.

For practicing or plunking, serious piano lighting

A music student can easily see to practice here, in a good balance of task and general light. The small brass lamp lights the score, while adjustable track spotlights mounted on a beam wash the area with a comfortable overall light level.

Making light of the competition

In this ping-pong room, serious matches take place under three utility fluorescent fixtures. Mounted side by side, they're dressed up and unified with a single redwood frame for a trim, finished appearance. Sliding door panels with similar trim glow with ambient light from another fluorescent fixture in the adjoining room. Architect: Kenneth Lim.

LIGHTING PICTURES, SCULPTURE, AND INDOOR PLANTS

You become the artist when you use light to help prints or paintings, a wall hanging, a piece of sculpture, or a favored indoor plant come to life.

Lighting pictures and other wall art

How you should light pictures and other artworks hung on the wall will depend on their textures and colors, and on how many items you wish to light at once. Photos of lighted wall art appear throughout the gallery section—pages 16–79.

Considerations of texture and color. To prevent shadows and reflections, a fixture—whether placed above or below—should bounce light off an artwork at a 30-degree angle. Decrease this angle if you want to highlight the surface texture of an oil painting or woven hanging. If a fixture generates a lot of heat, be sure to place it far enough away that it won't cause a picture's surface to deteriorate.

Though a wall painted a color other than white will spill some of that color onto artwork, the color can be neutralized by a filter on the art lighting fixture—a yellow filter, for example, will tone down the spill from a blue wall.

Artists' like to paint by light that's bluer than the light that most incandescent bulbs project. For this reason, you may wish to use pale blue filters on the fixtures you aim at paintings, in order to recreate the light in which the artist originally worked. (Some fluorescent bulbs simulate daylight, but they can't be aimed at a picture unless placed on its frame or just above it, as described below.)

Lighting individual pictures. The most precise—and costly—way to light a picture is with a framing projector. This device has adjustable shutters or a precisely cut template that shapes the beam of light to the exact shape and size of what's on the wall. Surface-mounted or recessed, most framing projectors take a 100-watt, long-life tungsten halogen bulb.

Less expensive and requiring fewer fine-tuning adjustments than a framing projector, a spotlight fixture will throw a beam on the picture and surrounding parts of the wall. As a downlight, a spotlight is recessed or hung from a track or housing box on the ceiling. As an uplight, it is attached to a weighted base that has a cord and plug, and set on the floor, a table, or a mantel. Typical bulbs for use in spotlight fixtures are the 120-volt PAR-38, the 12-volt PAR-36, reflector floodlights (wide beams), and spotlights (narrow beams).

Longitudinal fixtures, attached to the top or bottom of a picture frame or to the wall just above or below it (see photo at right), should have an adjustable reflector and telescoping bracket to adapt to extra-thick frames. The fixture should be no shorter than half the width of the frame. These fixtures use either fluorescent tubes or tubular 25 or 40-watt incandescent bulbs on 9-inch centers.

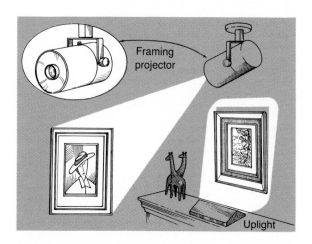

Lighting groups of pictures. If you have the money and patience to train individual lights on each picture in a group, use one of the methods just described.

A more economical way to light a group of artwork, though, is called "wall washing." Providing smooth illumination from ceiling to floor, wall washing makes a room look larger and lets you move pictures around without changing the lights.

Wall washing can be accomplished with evenly spaced canisters or other fixtures equipped with 150-watt R-type (internally reflecting) bulbs; or with tubular bulbs held in a reflecting, surface-mounted strip that has a lens plate to control light direction (see page 27). The farther from the wall you place the fixtures, the more subdued the texture of the wall will appear, and the more even the overall lighting.

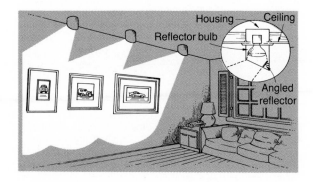

On-frame fixture beams light onto *Ancient Modern*.

Lighting sculpture

The difference between lighting pictures and lighting sculpture, of course, is that sculpture has three dimensions; it's the interplay of light and shadow that creates the overall effect. Any object—a seashell, a vase, an arrangement of flowers—may be lighted as though it were a piece of sculpture.

The larger the object, the more light it will need, but take care not to place a lighting fixture where it will bother people in the room. You can conceal downlights behind valances, uplights in vases or behind furniture, sidelights behind vertical strips of wood. To soften shadows, use fluorescent tubes; or establish a primary incandescent light source, then place a secondary light to throw its beams into the shadows created by the primary light (see drawing below). Photos appear on pages 23 and 27.

You can best determine the effect of light on a three-dimensional object by experimenting with one or more fixtures (see pages 40–41).

Lighting indoor plants

Think of plants as living sculptures: the artificial light that enhances their beauty should also help them grow. Photos of lighted indoor plants appear on pages 20, 22, 24, 35, 37, 41, 58, and 66.

Finding substitutes for sunlight. Though some bulbs supply the full color spectrum of sunlight, ordinary incandescent bulbs skimp on blue wavelengths, which promote foliage, and cool white fluorescent bulbs radiate few red wavelengths, which promote blossoms. Some plant lovers mix one watt of incandescence for every three watts of fluorescence—an ideal ratio.

It's also possible to purchase special incandescent or fluorescent "grow" bulbs, which provide the proper balance of blue and red light. Though more expensive than ordinary bulbs, grow bulbs eliminate the clutter of mixed incandescent and fluorescent fixtures.

If they receive no sunlight, most plants need 16 to 18 hours—but no more—of artificial light daily; an automatic timer will save you the trouble of remembering to turn lights on and off. If you use incandescent bulbs, keep them far enough away so that heat buildup won't brown the leaves.

Where to place lights. You can silhouette plants with concealed uplights, or by backlighting them against a luminous panel or lighted wall. Light bounces down through foliage when a fixture is recessed in or suspended from a ceiling. Wall-mounted or floor-standing fluorescent fixtures provide vertical light for vines or indoor trees.

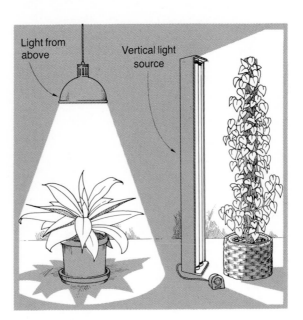

Elegant or informal, your dining area benefits from careful lighting. Sparkling light from a chandelier, combined with soft, indirect light on the walls and candles on the table, helps put your guests in a relaxed mood.

The main focus of dining room lighting should be the dining table, but a separate set of fixtures over your buffet supplies useful as well as ambient light at mealtimes.

Dimmers can be a real plus—turned up high, the light aids in the task of setting the table; on low, the gentle beam creates a festive atmosphere.

In order to dispel harsh shadows, augment downlights or opaque pendant lamps over the table with general light on the ceiling or walls.

Sophisticated ceiling sources

Three sleek bullet canister fixtures on a recessed track focus on the table in this contemporary dining room. Recessed wall-washer fixtures graze the wall with ambient light, highlighting the print. This type of ambient light counteracts the effect of strong downlighting above the table: it reflects a glow onto diners' faces, softening harsh shadows. Interior design: Nancy Glenn.

Variations on a romantic theme

Elegant dining under shimmering chandeliers has long epitomized romance. But the mood wanes when there's too little light on the tabletop for anyone to see what's being served. Now you can have your cake and see it, too, with chandeliers that feature concealed downlights. The upper photo shows only the "candles" on, for a gentle, twinkling light above the table. In the lower photo the downlights (usually limited to lower-wattage reflector bulbs) bathe the tabletop in light, making crystal and china gleam. With the chandelier hanging low enough (30 to 36 inches above the table is standard), there's little glare under any circumstances. Interior design: Nancy Glenn.

. . . DINING AREAS

Tiny lights twinkle between diners and sky

In this owner-designed solarium addition, tubes of low-voltage mini-lights are fastened to ceiling beams; two strips of molding nailed along either side of the tubes give a finished look. Along the original eave line runs a row of eyeball recessed lights—the most versatile fixtures available that would fit into the narrow space between ceiling and roof. Design: Steven Osburn. Interior design: Barbara Wolfe Interiors.

Glassware display and easy serving at a bright buffet

This European modular buffet unit was fitted with lights to accent glassware and illuminate the serving area. Tucked behind the faceboard at the top of each glass case, mini-tracks with tubular incandescent bulbs light all the shelves. Four small recessed downlights over the buffet hold 25-watt reflector bulbs. Both sets of lights are on dimmers, to provide an ambient glow when attention is focused on the table. A convenient plug-in outlet was also added at the right corner of the serving area. Design: Stanford Electric Works.

Sconce that's stunning in its simplicity

A half-bowl sconce accents the texture of reed wallpaper while providing ambient light for a gracious dining atmosphere. To achieve a feathery silhouette, an uplight can fixture is aimed at the wall from behind the plant. Interior design: Design Times Two.

A subtle quartet to dine by

Four deeply recessed downlights complement the oak furnishings in this clean-cut setting. With 50-watt PAR bulbs, fixtures on dimmers offer a wide range of levels, from bright light when used alone, as shown, to a subtle suggestion of light in combination with candles on the table. Inside the fixtures, metallic coating directs light in a controlled beam and cuts glare. On the left side of the ceiling, two recessed low-voltage spotlights are visible. They send light to accent artwork (not pictured) on a wall. Architect: Jack Woodson. Lighting design: James Cooper. Interior design: Design Professionals Incorporated.

Aura of light

The glow above this sliding glass door is repeated over the doors and windows throughout this house. The architects theorized that, because people are accustomed to daylight from doors and windows during the day, they'll be more comfortable with artificial lighting that creates a similar feeling at night. For indirect lighting, this design uses brackets with fluorescent fixtures. As the diagram below shows, the fluorescent fixtures are attached to the wall above the draperies. Two L-brackets bolted together support the faceboard; one bracket attaches to the wall, the other to the faceboard. Architects: Gary and Fani Danadjieva Hansen.

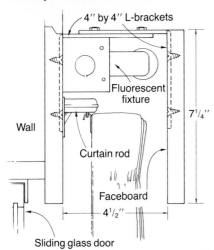

4″ by 4″ L-brackets

Fluorescent fixture

Wall

Curtain rod

7¼″

Faceboard

4½″

Sliding glass door

Track does the trick

To counteract the boxed-in feeling in this small living and dining room, both the table and the track lighting above it are on the diagonal. In combination with the painted diagonal line on the wall, this arrangement leads the eye to the longer angles of the room, making it seem larger. Light aimed onto the table gives it a sheen. The other fixtures are at work, too, lighting a print (not shown) and shedding general light over the sitting area. An uplight behind the Ficus casts delicate shadows on the ceiling. Interior design: Pamela Pennington.

Cut-glass and chrome chandelier

Echoing the triangular shape of the room's highest window, this owner-made chromed chandelier sparkles and shines above the table. Cut-glass beads, strung on stiff wires as shown in the drawing below, were handed down by a grandfather who handcrafted fixtures. Because they're clear, the four globe bulbs produce a light that sets the beads aglow.

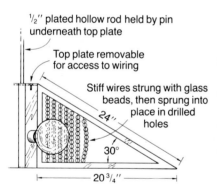

$^1/_2$" plated hollow rod held by pin underneath top plate

Top plate removable for access to wiring

Stiff wires strung with glass beads, then sprung into place in drilled holes

24"

30°

20 $^3/_4$"

Informal fixture combination

A combination of fluorescent and incandescent light makes this informal dining area inviting. A trough that supports fluorescent fixtures (see drawing below) runs the length of the room, bracketed to the wall at either end. Each fixture serves a definite purpose: the trough contributes a gentle, general light, and the pendant lamp directs its light onto the table-top. Because both fixtures are opaque, they create no reflection on the undraped glass doors.

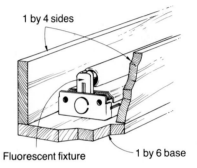

1 by 4 sides

Fluorescent fixture   1 by 6 base

Uncomplicated counter idea

For casual eating, a passthrough counter at the corner of this kitchen is illuminated with square recessed lights. These inconspicuous fixtures brighten the area without complicating its open lines or competing with the basket display. Cream-colored tiles reflect light from above, as well as that from the kitchen. Interior design: Ruth Soforenko.

EXPERIMENTING WITH LIGHT

It pays to know exactly what kind of light you want, and where it should be placed, before you invest in light fixtures for a room. The experimental light kit and accessories described here will help you make good lighting decisions at minimum expense.

The basic kit

For basic experimenting you'll need a standard utility clamp lamp with a standard conical aluminum reflector, a cylindrical make-it-yourself paper shade, a coffee can shade, a few bulbs, and one or more extension cords. Though you'll probably need only one or two such kits, you may want to invest in additional clamp lamps and cords, depending on how many new lights you're considering for any one room.

You'll also need a stepladder if you're planning ceiling fixtures.

Clamp lamp and cord. Available at most building supply dealers, a utility clamp lamp easily clasps the leg of a chair, the back of a couch, or an exposed beam overhead. Its swiveling clamp lets you point the light in any direction; both the clamp and the reflector can be removed to provide a simple socket, cord, and plug.

Translucent shade. To simulate the light-emitting qualities of a typical lampshade, place two $8^{1}/_{2}$ by 11-inch sheets of heavy white paper end to end. Lay strips of cellophane tape lengthwise along the seam on both sides.

Reinforce the two long edges of the resulting $8^{1}/_{2}$ by 22-inch rectangle by doubling over strips of tape lengthwise along the edges of the paper. Now tape the free ends of the rectangle together on both sides to form a paper cylinder 7 inches in diameter.

Spray both sides of the cylinder with fire retardant.

Tripod for shade. You'll need a tripod to secure the shade to the clamp lamp. To make the tripod, use wire cutters to snip the hooked end from a wire clothes hanger. Discarding the hook, straighten what's left with a pair of pliers, then bend the wire into the shape shown in the drawing.

Lay the tripod on top of the shade. Where the wire legs touch the shade, punch three holes in the shade about an inch below its top edge. Cover the holes on both sides with cellophane tape, then punch the holes again.

After unscrewing the reflector from the lamp's socket, snap the tripod in place.

Coffee can shade. A 2-pound coffee can approximates the size of many canister lamps. Punch a slot in the center of the bottom of the can with the tip of a screwdriver, then use wire cutters to remove a

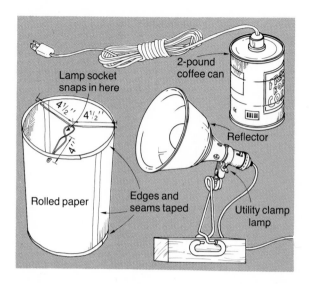

rough circle of metal slightly larger than the diameter of the clamp lamp's socket. A bulb screwed into the socket will hold the can in place.

What bulbs to use. You'll probably want to experiment with two types of bulbs, ambient and directional. Use ambient bulbs (standard household "A" bulbs) of 150 watts if you plan to add a dimmer to your experimental kit (see "Accessories," below); if not, use 60, 100, and 150-watt "A" bulbs.

Use three directional bulbs: an R-30 flood (widest beam), an R-30 spot (narrower beam), and a PAR-38 (narrowest beam). Buy 150-watt bulbs if you'll be using a dimmer, 75-watt bulbs if not.

Accessories

Several accessories expand the usefulness of the basic experimental kit. A 600-watt cord-mounted dimmer (shown on page 68) expands the range of illumination cast by your bulbs. Sheets of white, black, and colored paper, sprayed with fire retardant, can be used to line the inside surfaces of the two metallic shades, simulating the painted inside surfaces of many permanent fixtures. You may also want to make shades of colored paper to substitute for the basic white paper shade.

You can approximate the effect of fixtures hidden behind a cornice. To do this, cut 4 to 6-inch strips from cardboard cartons and attach the strips lengthwise to the ceiling with pieces of cellophane tape.

If human helpers aren't available, use cup hooks temporarily screwed into the wall or ceiling to hold clamp lamps and their cords.

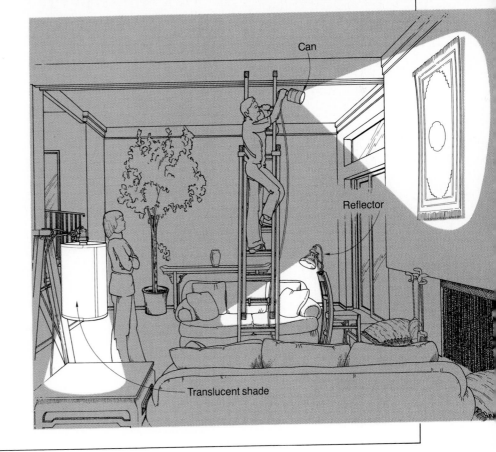

In the finished room, we can see the light at work. Carefully aimed track spotlights accent the oriental rug over the fireplace as well as the two plants. Next to the couch, a brass floor lamp produces a confined circle of strong task light. The table lamp in the foreground sheds a diffuse radiance over the whole corner of the room. In this case, all the fixtures chosen are highly flexible, allowing for additional decorative features or for basic rearranging. With the track lights on dimmers, the right light levels are available for a wide range of activities, from entertaining to reading by the fire.

In the planning stage, you can "move" your lighting by using these improvised fixtures, just as you move your furnishings around to achieve a comfortable, workable arrangement. The coffee can fixture affords you a kind of directional spotlight; the reflector produces a broader-beamed, more general light; and the paper shade projects a soft, diffuse type of light. By experimenting, you can find the exact lighting effects you want to complement your furnishings and lifestyle. Once you've seen what the right lighting can do, you can look for fixtures that will produce the type of light you need.

Can

Reflector

Translucent shade

Often a gathering place, the kitchen benefits from general lighting for after-hours snacks or entertaining. And whether one cook is at work or you have a crew of kitchen helpers, task lighting over the sink and on the countertops and rangetop is essential.

You'll want strong, shadowless light right over each kitchen work area. In most cases, shielded strip lights under the cabinets are best to light the counter area, while direct downlights illuminate the sink and work islands. Light-colored countertops and walls add brightness, because they reflect light.

If your countertops are well-lighted, general illumination on the ceiling or walls need only be bright enough to ensure safe movement about the room. Whether you choose decorative or functional fixtures, remember that, because they're in the kitchen, you'll need to clean them often.

Glow over a cooking island

This suspended fluorescent tube fixture, mounted in short ceiling track lengths for easy adjustment, concentrates light on the cooking island. Broad circles of general radiance come from deeply recessed open ceiling fixtures fitted with ring baffles to control glare. Interior design: Nancy Glenn.

Well-lighted "garage"

Here's a perfect example of light where it's needed. In this appliance garage, the slim fluorescent fixture—not visible when viewed from normal standing height—spreads its crisp light over the area where the appliances are used. Wall at the back is painted white for good reflective quality. Interior design: Nancy Glenn.

Skylight at center stage

Bright and cheery, with light where it's needed and wanted, this kitchen features an artificially illuminated skylight for a soft, diffused glow after the sun goes down (see drawing at left below). Countertop lighting comes from slim undercabinet fluorescent fixtures, while the sink counter receives light from glass-covered, easy-to-clean recessed fixtures. Architects: Michael D. Moyer and Lyle Mosher. Interior design: Janet Wasson Interiors.

Trough overflows with soft, shadow-free light

A continuation of the fluorescent light trough seen in the eating area on page 39 provides soft, indirect general light in this kitchen. Though the work surfaces are absorptive wood tones, light colors used on walls and cabinets reflect the light shed by fluorescent fixtures onto the countertops.

Fluorescent fixtures on all four sides of box

Skylight

18"

Ceiling

Spring latch

Piano hinge

Diffusing panels swing down for access to tubes

Side view

Spotting the problem

A single spotlight solves the problem of lighting the cooktop without interrupting this kitchen's open look. A short track provides light in the laundry area behind the cooking equipment. Design: Joseph Larocque.

Polished product of a household handyman

This handsome brass-bound butcherblock shelf serves three purposes—beautifully. It acts as a display platform for a collection of shiny cookware and green plants while supporting lighting fixtures and hiding the necessary wiring. Brass fixtures adjust to illuminate cooktop or countertop. As shown in the drawing below, wires originating in the ceiling run down through the brass pole and then through a channel routed in the butcherblock's top. This arrangement eliminates unsightly wires that might interfere with items displayed on top.

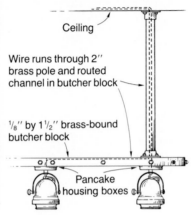

Ceiling

Wire runs through 2″ brass pole and routed channel in butcher block

1/8″ by 1 1/2″ brass-bound butcher block

Pancake housing boxes

Not a spot left unlighted

If a shallow ceiling prohibits use of recessed lighting, as it did here, use track or single spotlights. A row of track fixtures lights cabinets along the wall, and a series of deep can fixtures sheds work light over the countertops. In a sitting area at the far end of the room, glass sconces add a sparkling touch. Architect: Charles Moore. Lighting design: Richard Peters.

Pendant lamps position the light

Colorful industrial pendant lamps spread pools of light directly over the work island and dining table, creating cozy focal points in this high-ceilinged room. Silver-tipped incandescent bulbs reduce glare from the open fixtures. Undercabinet fluorescent fixtures and an open recessed downlight over the sink shed additional task light. Architect: Pamela M. Seifert.

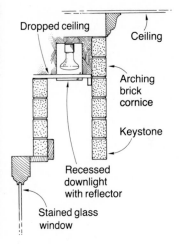

Dropped ceiling

Ceiling

Arching brick cornice

Keystone

Recessed downlight with reflector

Stained glass window

Curving brick conceals sink downlights

In this handsome renovation of an older home, rich, dark colors in the lower portion of a south-facing stained glass window serve to cut down glare during the day. At night, two recessed downlights installed behind a brick cornice (shown in the drawing at right) bathe the sink area with light. Design: Design Times Two.

Reflection upon reflection

Cherry red lacquered cabinets reflect
and repeat the double neon rectangles
used to provide low general light and
high visual interest in this kitchen.
Plenty of strong task light for the
countertops comes from slim fluorescent fixtures under the cabinets. A
convenient series of electrical outlets
on a strip has been built in at the
back of the counter and disguised
with a matching lacquered veneer.
Lighting design: Luminae, Inc.
Interior design: Nancy Glenn.

Light travels up to the ceiling, down through the kitchen

Another unique way to achieve general lighting in a kitchen is shown here, as enameled metal scoop fixtures throw light onto the ceiling in this narrow kitchen. Light, natural wood cabinets and white tile counters serve as reflective surfaces, making the most of the indirect light. Incandescent strip lights, often used for shelf lighting, provide worklight over the counters. Architect: David Petta. Lighting design: David Malman.

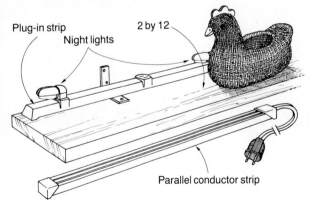

Plug-in strip

Night lights

2 by 12

Parallel conductor strip

Bright points spark a basket display shelf

Ambient light for informal kitchen gatherings can be provided by a shelf lighted like this. As the drawing at right shows, a plug-in strip or a parallel conductor strip fitted with nightlight fixtures can do a tidy job. Design: Bruce Velick.

SHEDDING LIGHT ON SHELVES AND CABINETS

Whatever objects your shelves and cabinets hold, carefully designed lighting will give them a life of their own. Objects may be washed or accented by light, from visible or concealed fixtures. Glass shelves, luminous shelves, and cabinets with glass doors offer special lighting opportunities.

Basic lighting techniques

Choosing from a variety of techniques and fixtures, you can light a wall of shelves or a single shelf—even focus on a solitary small object.

Ambient lighting. With this technique you can bathe one or more shelves in light from above, from the side, or from behind. Tubes or panels of light produce a more uniform glow than regularly spaced canisters. Especially suited for book and record collections, ambient lighting allows you to alter the arrangement of a collection without changing the position of light fixtures.

Shining light down from the ceiling may cause some shelves to cast shadows on the shelves below. Backlighting, vertical lighting from the sides, or tubes or mini-tracks attached under the front edges of shelves will eliminate this problem.

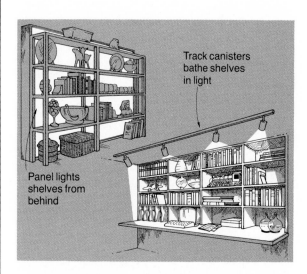

Track canisters bathe shelves in light

Panel lights shelves from behind

Accent lighting. Like ambient lighting, accent lighting on individual items can be accomplished from several directions (see drawing above right). A spotlight mounted behind an object will silhouette it. Light from a clip-on or track-mounted canister, focused from the side or just above an object, will emphasize the object's three dimensions. Low-voltage fixtures are useful for pinpointing small items, especially from a distance.

Sidelight

Light from behind

Downlight

Unless you use framing projectors (see page 30), ceiling lights are not recommended for accenting objects on shelves.

Concealed fixtures. Keeping the glare out of people's eyes and simplifying the look of a shelved display are the main reasons for concealing fixtures (see photo on facing page). Strips of wood attached to the edge of shelves will hide mini-track or fluorescent lights. Some shelves are built with strips of wood on all sides, to hide side or top-mounted accent lights.

Surface-mounted ceiling lights are easily concealed by a valance, recessed ceiling lights by a plastic or wood grid or a plastic diffuser panel.

Lighting glass shelves

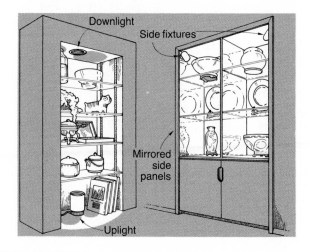

Downlight

Side fixtures

Mirrored side panels

Uplight

Wrapping around wall, bracket lights books.

Glass shelves create special opportunities for using light dramatically. By mounting fixtures directly above or below a stack of shelves, you send light up or down all the way through the stack. Especially rich effects can be created by beaming light through the stack in both directions.

If your glass shelves are encased in wood or recessed in the wall rather than set out on brackets, consider adding mirrors to the side panels. Mount an accent lighting fixture at each side either above the top shelf or below the bottom shelf, and aim the light at an angle.

Glassware and small objects like figurines are ideally suited for display on glass shelves. Fine platters or other flat objects should be tilted upright.

¼" acrylic or plate glass (set loose on top)

1" by 4" molding (grooved adapter cover to hold top and bottom panels)

Fluorescent tubes

Shelves that contain their own light sources can be built to illuminate what's below or nearby, too.

Hollow shelves containing fluorescent tubes need be no more than 2 inches thick. The drawing below left shows how to make one type of shelf. Top and bottom panels can be made of clear or translucent acrylic or glass. Support the shelf on wall brackets, or by screwing its wood fascia to vertical side panels and to wall studs.

Thicker luminous shelves (often called "light boxes") can be decorative as well as functional.

Lighting cabinets

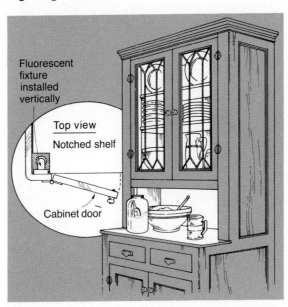

Fluorescent fixture installed vertically

Top view

Notched shelf

Cabinet door

Cabinets meant for displaying objects usually have glass doors. Such cabinets are most easily lighted by a fluorescent fixture installed vertically along each side of the shelves just behind the door frame (see drawing above). Notch out the shelves' front corners before mounting.

If you wish to accent objects rather than bathe them in light, use mini-tracks with pinpoint fixtures (see "Accent lighting" on facing page) instead of fluorescent tubes.

The contents of cabinets with solid doors need light only occasionally. Mount fixtures in this kind of cabinet as you would in a glass-door cabinet, but connect them to a pressure or limit switch (the kind used in refrigerators). Pressure switches are available from most electrical supply retailers.

See "Lighting glass shelves" (facing page) for ways to dramatize the interiors of cabinets that have glass shelves.

Whether your work area is a sewing room, a woodshop, or a drafting table, you'll need enough light to see easily—and you'll want to place the light carefully, so that your work surface is free from shadows. With a combination of general lighting and adjustable task lighting, you can avoid strong contrasts between a specific work area and the rest of a room.

If your surroundings have a high reflectancy, task areas will be easier to light: light-colored blotters on dark-finished desks and light-hued walls above workbenches or sewing tables reflect light back onto the work area.

For information on the levels needed for task lighting, see pages 6 and 8–9. A chart on page 8 gives recommended footcandle levels.

Shadowless sewing and laundry light

An expanse of white countertop stands ready for even the most ambitious sewing project. A 10-foot-long fluorescent tube hidden under the shelf floods the work surface with shadowless task light. Just a few steps away, the laundry area is also outfitted with fluorescent fixtures. Architect: David Jeremiah Hurley.

Easy-on-the-eyes sewing room

Flooded with daylight from three sides during the day, this sewing and craft room is also easy to work in at night. White ceiling and walls reflect the fluorescent fixture's even light onto the work counter. Adjustable track spotlights can be focused on an ironing board for the all-important pressing. Architect: Kenneth J. Abler.

Laundry made luminous

This upstairs laundry room is planned for action—the children even do their painting and crafts here—and the necessary light is supplied economically by fluorescent fixtures that don't get in the way. The ceiling fixture spreads general light throughout the room, while long, slim fixtures under the cabinets illuminate the laundry area on this side of the room and a desk-countertop on the opposite side. Architect: Michael Moyer. Interior design: Patricia Rubin.

Twin floor lamps light an artist's work table

Matching brass floor lamps over this artist's table adjust easily to light whatever work is in progress. General light comes from a globe ceiling light above (not pictured). Matchstick shades over the east-facing window reduce glare but let a small amount of light through.

Built-in lighting for a built-in desk

Neatly tucked into an alcove, this kitchen desk is flooded with task light by an undercabinet fixture installed above the white desktop. A wall bracket, which traces the perimeter of the room, spreads light down on the warm cedar paneling as well as upward to the ceiling. Architect: Kenneth J. Abler.

Open, bright, and ready for writing

The crisp lines of this desk area, where everything's within easy reach, are conducive to getting things done. A long fluorescent fixture fills the whole white desktop area with worklight. Above, three small recessed downlights illuminate the bookshelves' contents and add a softer incandescent tone to the work area. Architect: David Jeremiah Hurley.

A studied lighting scheme

In this handsome study, designed for nighttime bookkeeping, 200 foot-candles of light fall onto the desktop from the recessed spotlight above. Two more spotlights are stepped back on either side, to light the file drawers when they're opened. A series of wall-washer fixtures illuminate the bookshelves and add to the room's overall light level. Lighting design: Luminae, Inc.

Soy-tub ceiling fixtures

For a homeowner whose hobby is making wine, this wine cellar definitely ranks as an essential work area. Handmade recessed downlights are made (as shown in the drawing below) from soy tubs, cut in half and treated on the inside with a high-gloss finish to reflect light. Each one has a 325-watt globe bulb for a good measure of general light. Additional fixtures, hidden behind the ceiling beams and wired with dimmers, spread an indirect glow over the wine racks.

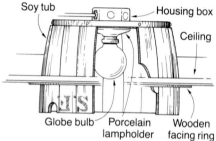

Soy tub
Housing box
Ceiling
Globe bulb
Porcelain lampholder
Wooden facing ring

On the right track

Two sets of track lighting with separate purposes brighten this basement woodworking shop. One track holds three 75-watt reflector floodlight bulbs and one 250-watt reflector bulb, principally for light. The other track is equipped with three 250-watt heat lamps to provide warmth and to shorten the drying time involved in laminating, gluing, and refinishing projects. Architect: J. Alexander Riley.

Basement workshop under lights

Sunny yellow pendant lamps with 100-watt bulbs provide color as well as overlapping circles of strong, concentrated task light in this basement shop. Recessed fixtures with wide beams spread a high level of general light through the room for less demanding activities.

ROOM-BY-ROOM IDEAS **57**

With a full staircase—or even just two steps down to another level—it's important to provide adequate light for safety. The nose or edge of each tread and the depth of each step should be clearly defined. One of the best ways to achieve this is to combine a direct downlight fixture over the stairs (to light the edges) with a softer light projected from the landing below (to define the depth of the stairs). In choosing and placing fixtures, be sure they won't direct any blinding glare into the eyes of people anywhere along the stairway.

Another option in lighting stairs is to build low-voltage fixtures into the wall just above every third or fourth step. Lights hidden in a handrail are also an unobtrusive but effective way to light the tops of stair treads.

Turn the page for a look at an entry hallway with well-lighted stairs.

The sum of several sources equals exceptional lighting

Grape ivy decks a lighted plant shelf (left) at the top of the stairs in this hillside house. Light on the ceiling above the plants comes from a single bulb in a simple ceramic fixture; a recessed downlight can illuminates the entry and landing. As shown below, low-voltage marine lights, designed for rough treatment in boats and buses, define every other stair tread. The open staircase gets its general light from the high-ceilinged living room. Architect: David Petta. Lighting design: David Malman.

Mini-lights outline each step

Plushly carpeted stair treads seem to float on layers of light that provide both a clear view of the edge of each tread and precise perception of the depth of each step. The cross section below shows how quarter-round molding nailed to each stair nose shields the low-voltage mini-lights. Risers were painted white and left uncarpeted to allow light to spill out. To avoid dimming due to voltage drops, each line of lights connects directly to the transformer. Lighting design: Randall Whitehead.

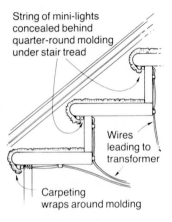

String of mini-lights concealed behind quarter-round molding under stair tread

Wires leading to transformer

Carpeting wraps around molding

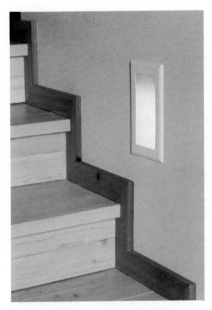

Unobtrusive, energy-saving wall panels

Easy to add in new construction, this type of illuminated plate fixture does its job safely and unobtrusively. Using minimal energy, the low panels can be left on all night to provide enough light for safe navigation. They may be the perfect solution for a short stairway between two house levels. Architect: J. Alexander Riley.

Light at your fingertips

For a compact, efficient solution to stair lighting, a fluorescent tube is hidden behind a slim handrail. Fluorescent tubes are well suited to this use—they don't produce much heat, so there's no danger of getting burned. Architect: David Jeremiah Hurley.

HALLWAYS / Follow well-lighted walkways

Hallways can be slim passage-ways, inviting galleries, or even open, glassed-in spaces. But as routes for human traffic, they should be neither much dimmer nor much brighter than adjoining rooms, so that your eyes don't have to make radical adjustments when you're going from room to room.

For safety, switches to control the lights should be at both ends of a hall. Ceiling or wall fixtures can aim light onto the walls or floor without getting in the way, even in the narrowest hallway. You'll want to provide light for any closets along a hall, either from inside or by directing a ceiling fixture at the door.

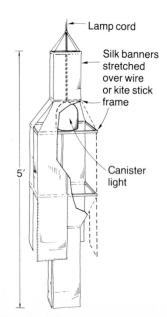

Lamp cord

Silk banners stretched over wire or kite stick frame

Canister light

5'

Lanterns lead the way

Sun-filled by day, this hallway is lighted for a soft nighttime look. Pairs of wall fixtures illuminate the floor and steps, and send a glow of light upward. A pin-hole aperture spotlight high on the wall highlights the trailing plant. Two custom-made kite lanterns (right) sway gracefully as they fill the hall with light. Architect: Charles Moore. Lighting design: Richard Peters. Lantern design: Charles Moore and Christina Beebe.

Lights wash paintings and passageway

The blue linen walls of this gallery hall are washed by recessed eyeball ceiling fixtures, inviting guests to look at paintings as they pass through. Interior design: Ruth Soforenko.

60 ROOM-BY-ROOM IDEAS

Angled tracks follow the maze

A mazelike passage full of angles posed a real problem in this older house. A line of track lights, broken into lengths to complement the angles, makes a handsome solution. Aimed at each painting and doorway along the way, fixtures provide all the light that's needed. Interior design: Jane Simons.

Extension into adjacent hallway

A sense of architectural continuity arises here from the long fluorescent tube fixture that seems to extend through the wall from the family room into the adjacent hallway. The two separate tube fixtures have a special reflector like the one on page 27, producing a high, even light · level. The hall glows with brightness as light is distributed further by white walls. Because of the lighting's indirect quality, there's little problem with glare on the prints along the wall. Architects: MLTW/Turnbull Associates. Lighting design: Richard Peters.

Bedroom lighting requirements range from the subtlest to the brightest. On the subtle end of the scale, soft levels create a quiet aura. Bright—but separate and adjustable—reading lights on either side of a double bed allow one person to sleep while the other reads into the wee hours.

A switch by the bed to turn off the main room light is handy.

You may want to include a light in front of a full length mirror, but remember: the light should shine on the person, not on the mirror. Lights in front of the bureau and inside closets aid in clothes selection.

Over-the-bed soffit

An unusual type of soffit lighting appears in this strikingly remodeled bedroom. The upper wall—from the ceiling down to a height of 6 feet—extends out far enough to accommodate a series of lights mounted as shown in the drawing below. Covered with an eggcrate grille to control glare, each 75-watt bulb sends a gentle fan of radiance down over the wall. Ceramic table lamps at either side of the bed add reading light and design interest as light and shadow play on their bases. Interior design: Ruth Soforenko.

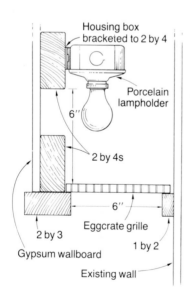

Housing box bracketed to 2 by 4

Porcelain lampholder

6"

2 by 4s

6"

Eggcrate grille

2 by 3

1 by 2

Gypsum wallboard

Existing wall

Inviting light to relax by . . .

Lighted by recessed downlights, the window seat in this bedroom extends an invitation to relax awhile. Open recessed downlights in a larger size illuminate the closets and bureau area for ease in clothing selection. Thanks to dimmers, both sets of lights produce a broad range of light levels—for atmosphere or activity. Lighting design: Luminae, Inc.

. . . and effective light to read by

In the room shown at left, matching wall-mounted lamps flank the bed-side as reading lights. Each has its own on-off switch and an extension arm that adjusts to fit personal reading habits.

Ceiling-suspended basket lamps

Striking lamps suspended on either side of this bed free the tops of the bedside chests. The lamps are adjustable, with pulleys for raising and lowering them. Inverted cane baskets envelop two standard glass globe fixtures. With a 75 or 100-watt bulb in each globe, the lamps supply plenty of light for reading or studying. Constructed as the drawing below shows, each lamp also has a control switch on a cord that drops down to the bed along the upright beam. Architect: J. Alexander Riley.

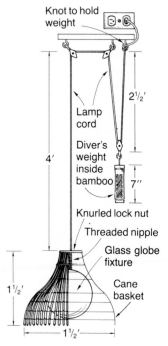

Knot to hold weight

Lamp cord

Diver's weight inside bamboo

Knurled lock nut

Threaded nipple

Glass globe fixture

Cane basket

2½'

7"

4'

1½'

1½'

Reading lamps built into the headboard

Warm scallops of light from inside this freestanding headboard stand in for separate reading lamps. In the dressing area beyond, recessed downlights illuminate grooming activities. Architect: Phoebe Wall.

Indirect lights for a relaxing atmosphere

Dramatic indirect lighting creates a relaxing atmosphere in this bedroom. A strip of low-voltage mini-lights tacked underneath outline the bed-frame and send a glow of light onto the hardwood floor. The rice paper screen diffuses soft blue light from a spotlight with a blue filter. Another uplight glows behind the pillar, while the shimmer of the globe light at the window is reflected on the warm-toned wooden chest. Lighting design: Randall Whitehead.

Designed for a teenager's private domain

Planned with a teen-age daughter in mind, this bedroom serves as a cozy place for record playing, chatting with friends, and reading textbooks, as well as sleeping. A wall bracket built into the shelf unit houses a series of tubular incandescent bulbs. The light level on these can be dialed with a dimmer, from atmospheric low to industrious high. A brass lamp with milky shade and adjustable base provides good reading light at the head of the bed. Interior design: Barbara Wolfe Interiors.

Pace-setting track plan

This inviting white room is lighted with three short track systems, one of which is shown here. Each of the carefully planned systems has its own particular area and purpose. Two of the spotlights here are aimed as accent lights—one at the painting and one at the plant. The other two add a wash of light on the daybed lounging area.

Shedding light on the sartorial subject

On the subject of dressing, these two deeply recessed ceiling fixtures take a clear stand. Their wide beams reach into the closets to help in selecting clothes and provide plenty of glare-free light for a final check of attire in the full-length mirror. Architect: David Jeremiah Hurley. Interior design: Jill Chozen.

Clearly illuminated closet

Lighting the way to easy clothing selection is a small track unit mounted high above the door in this orderly closet. Fitted with small fluorescent fixtures that burn cool and don't use much energy, the fixture is controlled by a switch on the outside of the closet. Architect: David Jeremiah Hurley.

LAMPS YOU CAN MAKE

Many familiar objects can be made into attractive lamps. We present four ideas here; see "Lamp wiring," page 85, for help in developing other projects.

Hanging balloon lamp

Wrap a blown-up balloon in plain or colored glue-soaked yarn to create a chandelier.

To make the shade, first suspend an inflated round balloon (3-inch diameter before inflated) above newspapers to catch glue drippings. Wipe a thin film of petroleum jelly over the balloon. Pour 8 ounces of white glue into a bowl and dilute with 4 ounces of water. Then soak about 5 ounces of loosely wound rug yarn in the glue.

Next, take one end of the string and slowly pull the whole length between your fingers to remove excess glue. Wind all the yarn around the balloon, leaving an oval opening, $2^3/_4$ by $3^1/_4$ inches, at the top and a 3-inch-diameter round opening at the bottom. After the yarn has dried overnight, pop the balloon; spray the shade with fire retardant.

To create a working plug-in fixture, cut a piece of round white SVT 2-wire electrical cord long enough to reach a plug-in outlet, plus 24 inches.

Following the drawing, connect the bare ends of the wires to the terminal screws inside a $1/_8$-inch threaded porcelain socket. Push the other end of the cord through a $2^1/_2$-inch-long threaded nipple. Screw the nipple into the top of the socket, tighten the set screw, and insert a 25 or 40-watt frosted tubular bulb. Place inside the shade.

Now slip a $3^1/_4$-inch vase cap onto the cord and slide it sideways through the top opening of the shade. Slip a second $3^1/_4$-inch vase cap onto the cord until it rests on top of the shade, and pull back on the cord until the two caps sandwich the shade between them. Slip a knurled lock nut over the cord and screw it onto the nipple to lock the caps in place. Screw on a cord-inlet bushing.

Attach a plug to the end of the cord; screw on an on-the-cord dimmer.

Inverted mixing bowl tops clay pipe lamp.

Clay pipe table lamp

A length of clay sewer pipe serves as the base and an enamel mixing bowl as the shade for this foot-high lamp. The mixing bowl's white interior helps reflect the light.

At a building supply store, buy a piece of 4-inch inside-diameter sewer pipe cut 5 inches long. The mixing bowl should be 10 inches in diameter and $3^1/_2$ inches deep. You'll also need 8 feet of lamp cord, a plug and an on-the-cord dimmer, a $4^1/_2$-inch-diameter porcelain lampholder, and a bulb adapter and tripod to hold the shade.

Before assembling, use pliers to nibble out a notch at one end of the pipe for conveying the cord from inside the pipe (see drawing). Wire the stripped ends of the cord to the screw terminals in the socket, and attach the plug to the other end. Install the switch at a convenient point along the cord. Use white glue to secure the lampholder to the "top" end of the pipe. Screw in a 60 or 75-watt bulb, snap on its adapter, screw on the tripod, and settle the shade.

A felt pad beneath the lamp's base will protect tabletops.

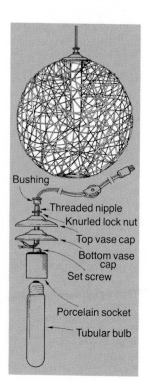

Bushing
Threaded nipple
Knurled lock nut
Top vase cap
Bottom vase cap
Set screw
Porcelain socket
Tubular bulb

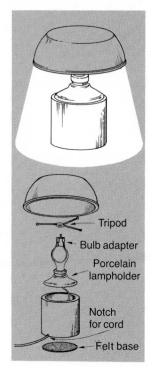

Tripod
Bulb adapter
Porcelain lampholder
Notch for cord
Felt base

Box kite floor lamp

A shade of white linen or unbleached muslin crowns this airy, easy-to-build floor lamp. To construct its frame, the only tools you'll need are a saw, drill, hammer, and screwdriver.

First cut four 54-inch lengths of $^3/_4$-inch-square molding for the legs. Cut six $17^5/_8$-inch lengths of $^1/_2$ by $^3/_4$-inch molding for the three cross braces at the top, bottom, and center of the frame. Notch both ends of these pieces with a triangular notch so the braces will fit flush against the legs (the distance between notch points should be $16^3/_4$ inches).

Assemble the top and bottom braces by crossing two pieces of wood and driving a brad through the center. Glue the ends of these braces in place 2 inches from the top and bottom of the legs. Cross the remaining two pieces of wood, drill a $^3/_8$-inch hole through the center, and insert a $1^1/_4$-inch length of threaded nipple into the hole in the center brace, securing it with two knurled lock nuts. Then glue the ends of this brace to the frame, $24^1/_2$ inches from the bottom of the legs.

Feed an 8-foot lamp cord up through the nipple and attach it to the socket as explained at right and as shown on page 85.

For the shade, cut a 32 by 56-inch piece of fabric. Fold over the long edges $^1/_4$ inch and press; then fold them over again $^3/_4$ inch, press, and stitch. Square the frame and wrap the material around it, hem side out; then mark for the seam line, on the raw edges at top and bottom. With the fabric's right sides together, sew the seam; then turn the completed shade right side out.

To keep the shade from charring, spray it on both sides with fire retardant, and use a bulb of no more than 75 watts.

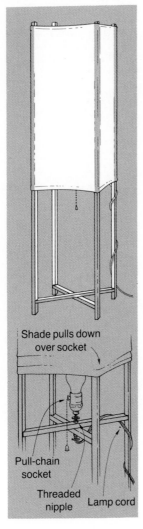

Shade pulls down over socket

Pull-chain socket

Threaded nipple   Lamp cord

Basket table lamp

Search in import, hardware, or gift shops for a basket with a lid and a stable base.

Begin by making a hole through the center of the top and bottom of each basket and through a side near the base.

Go to an electrical supply shop and buy the parts shown (except the upper part of the harp, which you'll buy later). You'll need a length of threaded nipple that equals the height of the basket *plus* the length of the decorative extender *plus* another $^1/_2$ inch for harp and socket connections. Don't forget 8 feet of lamp cord and a plug.

Push the nipple through the hole in the bottom of the basket and secure with a knurled lock nut. Then position another knurled lock nut on the nipple at a point that will be right under the lid when the basket is closed. Thread lamp cord through the nipple and out the basket's bottom, then side (if bottom is recessed), or just the side (if bottom is flat), as shown, leaving 3 inches of wire at the top to attach to the socket. Put on the basket lid, extender, harp base, socket cap, and socket; tighten the set screw to stabilize the socket.

Split the top of the cord down about $2^1/_2$ inches and tie an "Underwriters' knot" as shown. Peel $^1/_2$ inch of insulation from each of the two wires, twist and loop the ends clockwise around the terminal screws, and tighten the screws. Assemble the socket shell and push it down into the socket cap. Attach a plug to the other end of the cord.

Find a shade whose proportions please you, and then take the lamp *and* shade to an electrical supply shop and buy an upper portion for the harp that will hold the shade at the proper height.

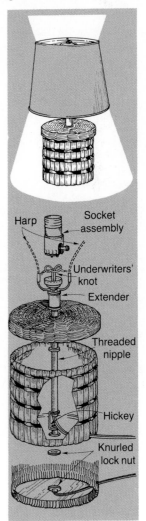

Harp

Socket assembly

Underwriters' knot

Extender

Threaded nipple

Hickey

Knurled lock nut

The trick to lighting bathrooms is to provide task light that's gently flattering and yet strong enough for grooming. Lights around a mirror used for shaving or putting on make-up should spread light over a person's face rather than onto the mirror surface. To avoid heavy shadows, it's best to place mirror lights at the sides, rather than only at the top of the bathroom mirror.

Consider dimmers here, too, to tone down the light level when it's not needed. In larger bathrooms, a separate fixture to light the shower or bath area and perhaps one for reading may be appreciated. And plan low-energy night lighting for safety, convenience, and decorative accent.

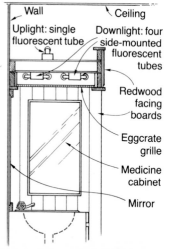

Up and down light

Doing double duty, a soffit variation adds height to this bathroom's cedar ceiling as it provides the mirror area with good, shadowless grooming light. The drawing at right shows the two separately operated sets of lights. Architect: Kenneth J. Abler.

Soffit lights the scene below

Mullioned soffit lighting in the bath is in keeping with the window trim in this remodeled older home. Fluorescent tubes mounted on the ceiling above the diffusing acrylic spread a strong, even light over the counter. The mirrored walls, often used with this type of soffit lighting, stretch the light further through reflection. Architects: Michael D. Moyer and Lyle Mosher. Interior design: Janet Wasson Interiors.

Stacked light sources

To save space in this small bath, the sink was recessed and a covered square downlight built in to light the washing-up area. The diffusing fixture above the mirror distributes an even radiance throughout the room. Architects: Michael D. Moyer and Lyle Mosher. Interior design: Janet Wasson Interiors.

Bright bars beside mirrors

Straightforward in design, light sources line up at the sides of these mirrors. Sidelighting is the most flattering and effective way to provide light at a grooming or make-up mirror. Though these incandescent tube fixtures are of European manufacture, similar fixtures made to operate on U.S. current are available. Architect: William Stout.

Luminous countertop creates low-key lighting

A luminous cultured onyx vanity countertop doubles as a unique, effective nightlight. Four 18-inch, 40-watt fluorescent tube fixtures—good choices because of their cool, energy-efficient light—were secured inside the cabinet (see drawing below). The designer chose cultured onyx because the fluorescent light's color reacted with some other countertop materials to produce an unattractive color tone. Design: Design Times Two.

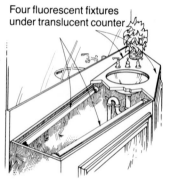

Four fluorescent fixtures under translucent counter

Boxlike mirror lights match cabinetry

Each of these handsome handcrafted bathroom lights houses two 60-watt incandescent bulbs in a double-ended socket fixture. The three-sided boxes, made of sheets of diffusing plastic and wood to match the cabinets, have been nailed directly to the wall. The top and bottom are open, both to allow easy changing of bulbs and to let the light spill out. Architect: J. Alexander Riley.

It's all done with mirrors

Mirror trickery in this small bath makes it seem spacious by reflecting light both from fixtures and from the white surfaces. Open ceiling fixtures, deeply recessed to avoid glare, provide most of the room's illumination. The low-wattage clear globe bulbs at either side of the mirror add enough light to soften any shadows from the downlights. Interior design: Nancy Glenn.

Theatrical bulbs star, with fluorescent tubes in a supporting role

Two sets of lights are at work here. For applying make-up, theatrical incandescent bulbs surrounding the mirror shed a flattering radiance on the face. Meanwhile, fluorescent tubes, hidden behind the wall bracket that extends around the room, spread a wash of light up to the ceiling and down over the paneled walls. Architect: Kenneth Lim.

Sparkling lines of mirror lights

Lines of low-voltage mini-lights set between mirror panels add sparkle and highlight the unusual angles of this bathroom. At night, with the other lights off, the tiny points of light provide a whimsical form of night-light. Recessed ceiling fixtures placed over the tub and each sink provide good overall lighting. Note the eyeball fixture trained on the painting in the reflection. Design: Design Times Two.

For good grooming, day or night

The sinks in this master bath suite face a north window to take advantage of natural daylight. At night, shiny blue Mexican tiles gleam with the radiance of two wide-beam recessed downlights. Twin mirrors swing out over the sinks for easy grooming. Architect: Michael D. Moyer. Interior design: Barbara Wolfe Interiors.

Tub in its own light

Designed for leisurely soaking, this tub has its own 75-watt light—on high, enough for reading; on dim, just enough to see by. A separate ceiling fixture above the steps has a 250-watt sunlamp to spread a pool of warmth for drying off. Architect: Michael D. Moyer. Interior design: Barbara Wolfe Interiors.

Family of frosted glass fixtures

Barely noticeable in this angular bath, a family of rectangular frosted glass fixtures provides diffused light in several essential areas. Shown at left, a single wall fixture provides reading light in the tub and toilet area, while a second sends its glow up, to be reflected by the white ceiling. On either side of the sinks (below), three rectangles combine to supply more intense but flattering light at the grooming area. Architect: Pamela M. Seifert.

Brass track highlights the tub

This handsome whirlpool tub is lighted by two brass track fixtures, one directed onto the tub, the other onto the access area. Track lighting isn't ordinarily used in bathrooms—the distance between the track and a water source is regulated for safety by a national code. With the track units off, there's still a soothing mood light glow at night: an outdoor fixture mounted under the house eave directs a gentle light onto the blinds at the window. Architect: Kenneth J. Abler.

Simplicity itself: double bulbs at the dressing table

On the far wall of the master bath shown at left, a bank of cabinets and drawers designed for neat storage also serves as a dressing table for the lady of the house. Warmed by the wood tones, the radiance of two 25-watt frosted globe bulbs provides plenty of light for the countertop. Architect: Kenneth J. Abler.

LIGHTING UP THE OUTDOORS

Plan outdoor lighting much as you would indoor lighting. It's easiest to begin by deciding where you'll need light at night for safety, activity, and security. Then you can add decorative or festive lighting—though in many cases you can choose lights that will be both functional and decorative.

No matter what kind of lighting you're working with, there are some basic considerations.

Beware of glare

Whether your lighting is decorative or functional, you'll want to avoid glare from your fixtures. In effect, glare is the reason for the discomfort we feel when looking at a light that's too bright, or one that's aimed directly at us. At night, because the contrast between darkness and a source of light is so great, glare can be a persistent problem. Several methods of minimizing glare are discussed below.

Use shielded fixtures. In a shielded fixture, the bulb area is completely hidden by an opaque covering that directs the light away from a viewer's eyes. The eye sees the warm glow of a lighted object rather than a hot spot of light. In the photograph at right, a simple shielded fixture directs its light downward over the doorway and doorbell-intercom. A translucent diffusing panel over the lower opening prevents glare from offending the eyes of a guest. Inside, along the solarium walkway, a number of frosted globe lights give an inviting glow.

Place fixtures out of sight lines. Another way to avoid glare is to place your fixtures either very low, as along a walk; or very high on a tree—and then direct them in such a way that only the light playing on the tree branches, and not a bright spot, is noticed.

Use lower light levels. Rather than using one high-wattage light at your front door, it's at once less glaring and more inviting to use several softer lights strategically placed in the front yard.

Low-voltage or standard current?

Low-voltage lighting systems are often used outdoors; the standard household voltage of 110 is "stepped down" to 12 volts by a transformer so that it isn't as strong—and there's less danger of shock. Low-voltage systems can also be more energy-efficient than 110. And the wires of a low-voltage system don't have to be buried and are therefore easier to work with. For more discussion of the two types of current, see pages 94–95.

In addition to the packaged low-voltage systems available, you can use low-voltage PAR spotlights with narrow or broad beams to light trees or larger areas. These spotlights provide strong light while using less energy than ordinary spotlights.

Lighting for safe movement

You'll want to look critically at several points on your property—along your driveway, front walk, and steps; around the front door and the backyard gate; on the deck or patio; around the swimming pool; and in planted areas—to make sure that both family members and guests will be able to move easily and safely even on the darkest night.

Driveways, especially if they're long and wooded, should have some kind of lights to define their boundaries, particularly around turns or along tricky terrain. Fixtures installed for this purpose should be low and soft enough to prevent glare in a driver's eyes. Reflectors attached to stakes or fences along the way can augment your electric lights. For shorter driveways, you may want only a light at the street to designate your driveway entry or light your house number.

Front walks and steps are easiest to light if they're made of a light, reflective color. Low fixtures that spread small, soft pools of light can greet guests and highlight your garden's virtues along the walk.

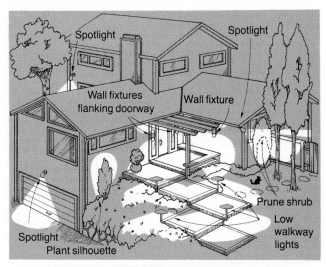

A balance of decorative and security lighting makes this home attractive and safe. The soft lights lead the way to the well-lighted front porch, while carefully placed spotlights delineate the yard's outer edges.

Series of lights invites guests into the house.

If your house has deep eaves or an overhang extending the length of your walk, you might consider installing weatherproof downlights to illuminate your walk and plantings without any visible fixtures.

Often your steps will be adequately lighted by fixtures at the front door, but even single steps should be illuminated if they're any distance from the door. A small fixture above the steps will do, though you may be able to build in a light under the stairs or along a wall or railing.

At the front door, you'll want light for several purposes. In addition to lighting your house number and welcoming your guests, you'll want light enough to see a caller's face. Often a front door light is above or to the side of the door. If you have only one light to the side, be sure that it's on the doorhandle side, so you can easily see to unlock the door when you're coming home. If you choose decorative clear glass fixtures, remember to keep low-wattage bulbs in them to avoid uncomfortable brightness.

Adequate lighting at the back gate and other house approaches gives a sense of security. You may wish to use spotlights mounted high on your house walls. As this kind of fixture directs a strong light,

you can aim it to graze a wall, illuminating the area without glaring directly in anyone's line of vision. Photocells are available that turn these lights on at dusk and off at dawn, to cut down on their high energy use as well as to provide security when you're away. As the drawing on the facing page shows, you may need to trim bushes that grow into the path of the light and cut down on its effectiveness. For more information on using lighting as a security measure, see page 12.

On patios and decks, a low level of light is often enough for quiet conversation or *al fresco* munching. By lighting steps, railings, or benches indirectly from underneath—or directly with strings of mini-lights—you can outline the edges of your structure for safety, too. For ease and safety in dining, don't forget to add a stronger light wherever you do your serving or barbecuing.

Consider temporary lighting for festive occasions: strings of lanterns, sparkling Christmas tree lights, hurricane lanterns, Mexican pierced cans for candles, or any safe, small lamps. To avoid using long extension cords, it's a good idea to install a few outlets on your deck or patio.

Swimming pools and spas require special consideration, too. These areas should be lighted for safety, and to make them attractive from inside the house. Most pools have an underwater light in the deep end. Consider putting this on a dimmer, especially if the light is in view of the house or patio sitting area, to avoid glare. For relaxing and entertaining, all the light that's needed is a soft glow to outline the pool edges, but the light should be on full brightness when children are swimming. Low spotlights muffled by foliage or trained on walls can provide dramatic indirect lighting, reflecting in the pool surface when the pool light is off.

Popular for an evening soak, a spa can be illuminated with low-voltage twinkling mini-lights that will outline its perimeter or steps without being bright.

When lighting a pool or spa—as when doing electrical work in all wet areas—make sure to check local electrical codes, and be sure that your transformers and outlets are properly grounded.

Lighting trees and foliage can be an effective way to mix functional and decorative lighting. Several lighting strategies can be used both to show off your plantings and to softly light a dark area. For a dappled, "moonlight" effect, place a spotlight high in a large tree. To highlight an interesting structure or texture, angle a light upward from below. To silhouette plantings, aim a spotlight at a fence or house wall from close behind the plants.

WIRING IT ALL TOGETHER

M A T E R I A L S • T O O L S • T E C H N I Q U E S

Here's an array *of lighting materials and tools—from tiny wirenuts to lengthy tracks. Installation techniques are explained on the following pages.*

Once you've analyzed your lighting needs (see pages 4–9) and learned about the various fixtures, bulbs, tubes, and controls available (see pages 9–15), you're ready for the next step: improving the lighting in your home. Whether you plan simply to replace an ON-OFF switch with a dimmer or to enhance an entire room with new fixtures, many of the how-to-do-it basics are the same.

This chapter will show you how to determine how much light (measured in watts) you can safely add to existing circuits, how to wire or repair plug-in lamps, and how to install dimmers, timers, fixtures, plug-in outlets, switches, and outdoor lights. If you need to do more than tap into existing circuits, consult the Sunset book, *Basic Home Wiring*, or see a licensed electrician.

Should you do your own work?

Doing your own electrical work may not always be the best idea. Your local building department may restrict how much and what kinds of new wiring a homeowner may undertake. If yours is an older home, for instance, and you discover that the wiring inside the walls is the old-fashioned knob-and-tube variety (see page 84), local regulations may require that new hook-ups be made by a licensed electrician.

Even if your locality doesn't restrict what kinds of electrical work you do in your own home, you may still wish to use the services of an electrician. If electrical problems crop up that you don't understand—or if there's any doubt in your mind about how to proceed with a home lighting project—it's best to call on a professional.

Codes and permits

If you want to do your own hook-ups, you should first talk with your building department's electrical inspector about local codes, the National Electrical Code, and your jurisdiction's requirements concerning permits and inspections.

The National Electrical Code spells out the wiring methods and materials to be used in all electrical work. The Code forms the basis for all regulations applied to electrical installations, and its central purpose is safety.

The information given in this book complies with guidelines set out by the National Electrical Code. Some cities, counties, and states amend the Code to suit their particular purposes, though, and as a result, specific regulations can vary from county to county and even from town to town.

Safety first

The most important rule for all do-it-yourself electricians is this: *never work on any electrically "live" circuit, fixture, plug-in outlet, or switch*. Your life may depend on it.

Before starting any work, you must disconnect the circuit you'll be working on at its source, either in the service entrance panel or in a separate subpanel. If your circuits are protected by fuses, simply removing the appropriate fuse will disconnect the circuit from incoming current. In a service entrance panel or subpanel equipped with circuit breakers, you can disconnect a circuit by switching its breaker to the OFF position.

To make sure that you disconnect the correct circuit, turn on a light somewhere along the circuit before you remove the fuse or turn off the circuit breaker. The light will go out when you've removed

the correct fuse or turned off the correct breaker.

If you have any doubt about which fuse or breaker affects which circuit, shut off *all* current coming into your home at the main disconnect (identified as MAIN). Usually the main disconnect is located at the service entrance panel, as shown below.

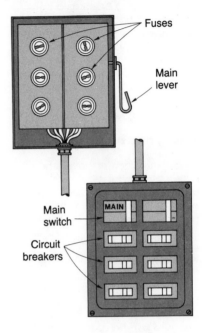

So that no one will come along and replace the fuse or reset the circuit breaker while you're working, tape a note to the panel that explains what you're doing. Then either carry the removed fuse with you in your pocket or tape the appropriate circuit breaker securely in the OFF position.

WIRE COLOR-CODING

For simplicity's sake, unless otherwise indicated, the wires shown in this book are color-coded as follows:
- Hot wires—thick black.
- Neutral wires—thick white.
- Grounding wires—narrow black.

Actual wires come in a greater variety of colors. Here are some of the wire or wire insulation colors you may come across:
- Hot wires—usually black or red, but may be any color other than white, gray, or green. (If a hot wire is white, it should be taped or painted black near terminals and splices for proper identification.)
- Neutral wires—white or gray.
- Grounding wires—bare copper or aluminum; green. (Grounding wires are rarely black.)

CIRCUITRY CONSIDERATIONS

The word "circuit" refers to the course an electric current travels, from the source of power (the service entrance panel or a subpanel wired to it) through some device using electricity (such as a light fixture) and back to its starting point, the source. What may appear to be a hopelessly tangled maze of wires running through the walls and ceilings of your home is actually a well-organized system composed of several circuits.

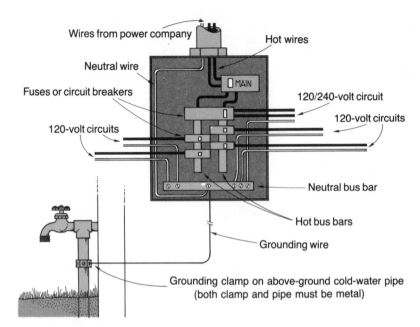

How your home is wired

Today, most homes have what's called three-wire service. The power company connects three wires to the service entrance panel. Each of two "hot" wires supplies electricity at 120 volts. During normal operation, the third wire, a neutral wire, is maintained at zero volts.

Three-wire service provides both 120-volt and 240-volt capabilities. One hot wire and the neutral wire can be used to complete a circuit for 120-volt needs, such as lights and plug-in outlets. Both hot wires and the neutral wire can be used to complete a circuit for 240-volt needs, such as an electric range or clothes dryer.

Many older homes have only two-wire service, with one hot wire at 120 volts and one neutral wire. Two-wire service doesn't have 240-volt capability.

Service entrance panel. The control center for your electrical service is the service entrance panel. Housed in a cabinet or box, it's often located outside your home, below the electric meter. It can also be on an inside wall, directly behind the meter.

In this panel you'll usually find the main disconnect (the main fuses or main circuit breaker), the fuses or circuit breakers protecting each individual circuit, and the grounding connection for your entire system.

Circuit distribution center. After passing through the main discon-

nect, each hot wire connects to one of two strips of metal, called "bus" bars, in the distribution center. These bars accept the amount of current permitted by the main fuses or circuit breaker, and divide that current into smaller units for the branch circuits, as shown above. The distribution center may be housed in the service entrance panel or in a separate subpanel, located elsewhere in the home.

Circuits for lights. In most homes, several light fixtures and plug-in outlets operate on the same circuit by what is called "parallel wiring," as shown below. The hot and neutral wires run continuously from one fixture or outlet box to another.

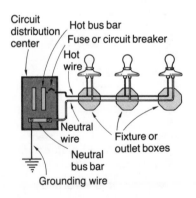

Wires or plug-in cords branch off from these continuous hot and neutral wires to individual lighting fixtures. Switches, timers, and dimmers (see pages 86, 88, and

93) are installed along the hot wire to control individual lights or groups of lights.

Grounding prevents shock. The National Electrical Code requires that every circuit have a grounding system. Grounding ensures that all metal parts of your home's wiring system will be maintained at zero voltage, for all are connected directly to the earth. In the event of a short circuit, a grounding wire carries current back to the circuit distribution center—rather than through the body of a person who comes in contact with the faulty circuit—and ensures that the fuse or circuit breaker will open, shutting off the flow of current (see drawing below).

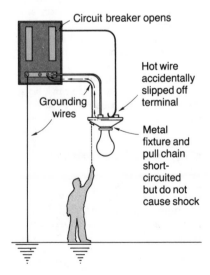

The nonmetallic sheathed cable (see page 84) used to tap into most circuits carries its own grounding wire. The grounding connection from an outlet box to a plug-in outlet (see page 92) is made with a short piece of wire screwed to the box. The screws that hold a metal fixture to its box ground the fixture (see page 87)—except with a chain-hung fixture, in which case a separate grounding wire is run from box to fixture (see page 88).

Mapping your circuits

If you plan to install additional lighting in your home (as opposed to simply replacing fixtures—see page 87), it's important to know which circuits control which existing appliances, fixtures, plug-in outlets, and switches. Some of these circuits may already be carrying the maximum current allowed by law (see "Calculating maximum watts" on this page).

To decode your wiring, start by giving a number to each fuse or circuit breaker in the circuit distribution center (if you have more than one subpanel, be sure to number all branch circuits). Next, draw a map showing every room, including the basement and garage. Using the symbols shown in the sample map below, indicate on your own map the approximate location of each appliance, fixture, plug-in outlet, and switch.

To chart the circuits, you'll need a small table lamp or night light that you can easily carry around with you to test all plug-in outlets. After turning the first circuit breaker to the OFF position or removing the first fuse, go through the house and check all appliances, switches, and plug-in outlets; on your map, label those that are now dead with the circuit number.

Repeat the process with each circuit, first making sure that you've turned the previous circuit breaker back on or replaced the previous fuse.

Calculating maximum watts

Once you've mapped your circuits, plan to add fixtures or plug-in outlets to those circuits controlled by 15-amp circuit breakers or fuses; adding lights to circuits that can carry more than 15 amps is often illegal. The number of amps is marked on each circuit breaker or fuse.

As a rule a 15-amp circuit can handle a maximum of 1440 watts. Add up the watts marked on the appliances and bulbs fed by the circuit you want to add to. The difference between this sum and 1440 is the total number of watts that you can add to the circuit.

If you're confused by load calculations, or if you want to know if you can tap into a circuit rated at more than 15 amps, call on your building department's electrical inspector. Take along your circuit map; a list of the appliances and bulbs currently serviced by the circuit in question, and their watt-

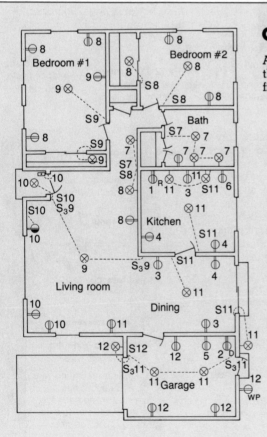

CIRCUIT MAPPING

At left is a circuit map of a typical two-bedroom house. Note that the dashed lines indicate which switch controls which fixture; they do not show wire routes.

Electrical symbols	Circuit identification
⊗ Light fixture	1. Range (50 amp)
⊖ Double plug-in outlet	2. Dryer (30 amp)
⊖ Double plug-in outlet, half controlled by switch	3. Kitchen and dining room (20 amp)
S Single-pole switch	4. Kitchen and dining room (20 amp)
S₃ Three-way switch (two switches control one fixture)	5. Washer (20 amp)
	6. Dishwasher (20 amp)
⊕R Range outlet	7. Bath and hall (15 amp)
⊕D Dryer outlet	8. Bedroom #2 (15 amp)
▭ Doorbell	9. Bedroom #1 (15 amp)
⊖WP Weatherproof plug-in outlet	10. Living room (15 amp)
	11. Living room (15 amp)
----- Switch wiring	12. Garage (20 amp)

ages; and a list of the fixtures and outlets you'd like to add, also rated according to their wattages.

WORKING WITH WIRE

With only a few tools and materials, and the knack of making splices, you can handle most wiring chores.

Six useful tools

In addition to common tools such as standard and Phillips screwdrivers and needle-nose pliers, the following specialized tools come in handy for doing electrical work.

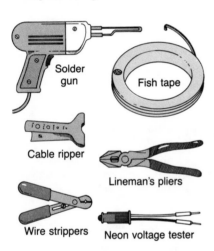

Solder gun

Fish tape

Cable ripper

Lineman's pliers

Wire strippers

Neon voltage tester

Lineman's pliers are an electrician's basic tool. Serrated jaws hold wires firmly, and just behind the jaws is a set of wire cutters.

Wire strippers are available in several designs, ranging from a simple two-piece scissors type to a complex self-clamping type.

Cable ripper rips the outer insulating sheath on nonmetallic sheathed cable, allowing you to peel away the insulation. Use this tool only on standard flat two-wire cable.

Fish tape is a must whenever you're going to pull wires through walls (see page 89). Made from long pieces of flattened spring steel, 25 and 50-foot fish tapes come on reels for easy handling.

Neon voltage tester determines which is the hot wire in a two-wire circuit with ground. You touch one probe to the grounding wire (or metal box) and the other probe to the other two wires, one at a time. The tester lights when the second probe contacts the hot wire. (Caution: Because a circuit must be left on for testing, keep your fingers off the probes' bare metal tips when using a voltage tester.)

Solder gun is needed only for splicing tie-ins to old knob-and-tube wiring (see "Splicing," at right), and can be rented.

Three vital materials

At most, you'll need only three types of materials—nonmetallic sheathed cable, wirenuts, and housing boxes for wirenut splices—to complete most interior wiring chores. Before you purchase any materials, be sure they conform to the requirements of your local building code.

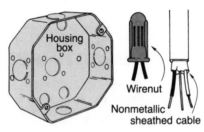

Housing box

Wirenut

Nonmetallic sheathed cable

Nonmetallic sheathed cable contains a hot wire (wrapped in black thermoplastic), a neutral wire (wrapped in white thermoplastic), and usually a grounding wire (bare or wrapped in green thermoplastic). To ensure the best splices, use only cable containing all-copper wire, not aluminum or copper-clad aluminum wire.

Wirenuts join and protect the stripped ends of spliced wires within housing boxes. Once you know how many wires of what size you'll be splicing together, you can get the proper sizes of wirenuts.

Housing boxes (or "boxes"), made of metal or plastic, are rectangular, octagonal, or square, depending on their purpose and how many wirenut splices they were designed to hold. Fastened within

the wall or ceiling, sometimes to wooden studs or joists, these boxes are usually capped with fixture canopies, outlet plates, or switch plates. More housing boxes are shown on page 89.

Splicing—easier than you might think

Most wire splices are made in housing boxes with wirenuts. If you discover that your home is equipped with old-fashioned knob-and-tube wiring (separate hot and neutral wires threaded through porcelain knobs and tubes), you may need to use a 250-watt solder gun. Both wirenut and soldered splices are discussed below.

Wirenut splices are easy to make. Start by stripping off an inch of insulation from the ends of the wires you're going to join. Hold the stripped ends together and snip off $3/8$ to $1/2$ inch from the wires so that the ends are even. Finish by screwing the wirenut on clockwise.

Soldered splices (copper to copper only) are required to carry current from hot and neutral knob-and-tube wires into a housing box, as shown below.

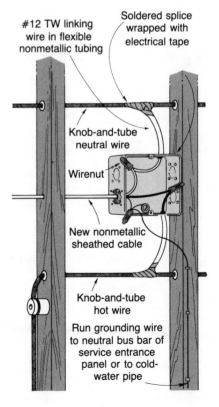

#12 TW linking wire in flexible nonmetallic tubing

Soldered splice wrapped with electrical tape

Knob-and-tube neutral wire

Wirenut

New nonmetallic sheathed cable

Knob-and-tube hot wire

Run grounding wire to neutral bus bar of service entrance panel or to cold-water pipe

Strip 2 inches of insulation from the knob-and-tube wire you want to splice, and 1½ inches from the end of the linking wire. Sand the wire ends with coarse-grained emery paper until shiny. Twist the bare end of the linking wire tightly around the bare knob-and-tube wire, forming a coil ¾ inch long, and snip off the stub end of the linking wire.

Heat the coil with a 250-watt solder gun, then touch the tip of a roll of rosin-core solder to the coil. You'll know that the coil has reached the proper temperature when the solder flows readily into the spaces within the coil but does not flow out again. Once the spaces are filled, take away the gun and the roll of solder.

When the liquefied solder has rehardened and the coil is cool, wrap the coil and the bare portion of the knob-and-tube wire with rubber insulation tape; seal the rubber insulation tape by wrapping it in the opposite direction with plastic electrical tape.

LAMP WIRING

Most plug-in incandescent lamps are electrically alike. If you're creating a typical table lamp from scratch (see pages 68–69), assemble it as shown in the drawing above right. If you're repairing a lamp, refer to the same drawing and the following instructions.

Troubleshooting a lamp

Here's how to diagnose the problems in a lamp that doesn't work:

1) Check the bulb to make sure it hasn't simply burned out, and that it's screwed in as far as it will go.

2) Plug the lamp into another outlet to be sure that the trouble is not with the outlet ordinarily used.

3) Check the lamp's cord and plug, and any extension cord being used, for breaks and frayed areas.

4) If everything else works, unplug the lamp and replace the socket unit (shell, sleeve, core, and switch), leaving the Under-

writers' knot and socket cap in place.

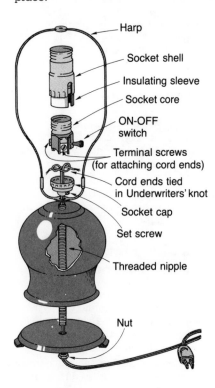

- Harp
- Socket shell
- Insulating sleeve
- Socket core
- ON-OFF switch
- Terminal screws (for attaching cord ends)
- Cord ends tied in Underwriters' knot
- Socket cap
- Set screw
- Threaded nipple
- Nut

Replacing a cord

Here are the six steps necessary for replacing an old cord with a new one:

1) Remove the socket shell by squeezing and lifting near the switch, where the word "Press" is embossed. Remove the insulating sleeve.

2) Noting which wire goes where, remove the old wire ends from the terminal screws, then untie the Underwriters' knot.

3) Stripping about ¾ inch of insulation from the new cord, twist the wires of the old cord and new cord together. Wrap electrical tape around the twisted wires.

4) Pull out the old cord from the bottom of the lamp while feeding the new cord through the lamp from above. When the new cord is in place, detach the old cord.

5) Tie an Underwriters' knot with the wires of the new cord; twist and loop the bare ends clockwise around the terminal screws and tighten the screws.

6) Push the socket shell into its cap until it clicks into place.

SURFACE WIRING

Where routing wire through walls is difficult, and cutting open walls, ceilings, and floors is not feasible (see page 89), surface wiring provides an alternative. Whether housed in plastic or metal, surface systems allow you to mount plug-in outlets, fixtures, and switches anywhere along a circuit, on practically any surface.

Though three systems of surface wiring are available, metal raceway is the most common. All three systems are very easy to install; instructions follow.

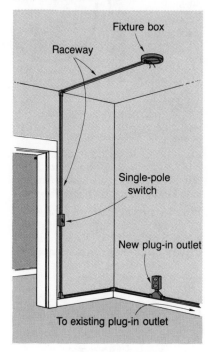

- Fixture box
- Raceway
- Single-pole switch
- New plug-in outlet
- To existing plug-in outlet

Metal raceway. Self-grounding flattened tubes snap into clips that have been screwed or bolted to the wall. Two #14 TW (thermoplastic-insulated) wires are then threaded through the tubes.

Before attaching raceway to a wall or ceiling, you'll need to wire its starting end to an existing plug-in outlet. Pull the outlet from its box, but leave the wires connected. After fitting the outlet into a raceway extension box, connect the raceway wires to the outlet as shown at the top of the next page. You may need to use fish tape (see page 84) to pull the wires through the raceway.

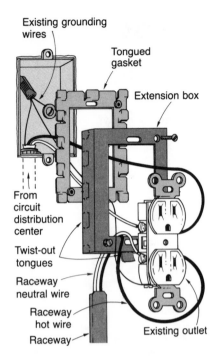

Existing grounding wires

Tongued gasket

Extension box

From circuit distribution center

Twist-out tongues

Raceway neutral wire

Raceway hot wire

Raceway

Existing outlet

Standard outlets, fixtures, and switches attach to raceway wires in the same way that they attach to in-the-wall wiring (though without the grounding wire), but they must be housed in raceway extension boxes, as shown above.

Wire-in strips. Much like the aluminum track lighting systems described on page 91, these rigid plastic strips have wires running under a lip along each side. A connector is wired into an existing plug-in outlet box.

Plug-in strips. These flexible plastic ribbons contain their own wires. A grounded, three-prong plug, inserted into a standard plug-in outlet, connects them to the house's present electrical system.

REPLACING SWITCHES WITH TIMERS OR DIMMERS

Most electronic timers and dimmers can be wired into existing circuits in the same way as the switches they replace. This holds true whether the timers and dim-

mers were made to control 120-volt incandescent bulbs or to control low-voltage incandescent bulbs with transformers built into the fixtures.

A timer for a fluorescent tube is installed in the same way as a timer for an incandescent bulb, but installing a fluorescent dimmer involves more steps.

On these two pages we tell you how to replace the two common types of switches with timers or dimmers, and how to dim fluorescents.

Before starting, don't forget to cut off power to the switch you'll be replacing.

Installing timers and incandescent dimmers

Usually a single switch controls a light or group of lights; this type of switch is called a single-pole switch. It must be replaced with a single-pole dimmer or timer.

Sometimes two switches control a light or group of lights, as at the top and bottom of a flight of stairs. Such switches are called

three-way switches. If you want to add a timer or dimmer to such a system, replace the three-way switch most often used with a three-way timer or dimmer, and leave the second three-way switch in place.

The drawings below show the two ways a single-pole switch may be wired into your home, and the two ways a three-way switch may be wired. After you've unscrewed the switch plate and switch mounting screws and pulled the switch from its housing box, detach the wires from the terminals on the switch, and reattach them to similar terminals on the timer or dimmer. (On three-way switches, timers, and dimmers, one of the three terminals will be marked "common." Be sure that the wire attached to the common terminal on the switch being replaced is reattached to the common terminal on the timer or dimmer.)

If the timer or dimmer comes with short wires instead of terminals, use wirenuts to splice their free ends to the wires in the switch box (see drawing at right top).

Single-pole switches

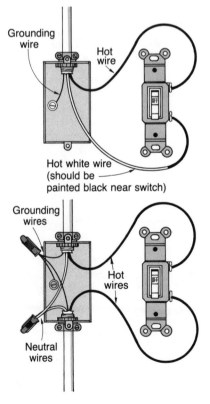

Grounding wire

Hot wire

Hot white wire (should be painted black near switch)

Grounding wires

Hot wires

Neutral wires

Three-way switches

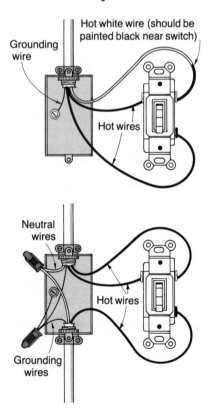

Hot white wire (should be painted black near switch)

Grounding wire

Hot wires

Neutral wires

Grounding wires

Hot wires

Three-way timer or dimmer with its own wires attached

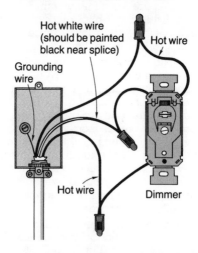

Hot white wire (should be painted black near splice)

Hot wire

Grounding wire

Hot wire

Dimmer

Installing fluorescent dimmers

If you want to install a dimmer for a fluorescent fixture, first make sure the fixture is equipped with

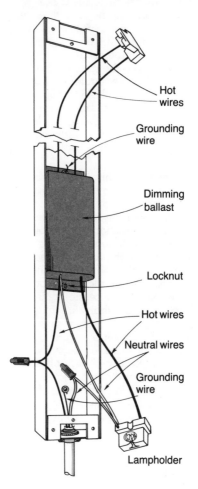

Hot wires

Grounding wire

Dimming ballast

Locknut

Hot wires

Neutral wires

Grounding wire

Lampholder

rapid-start tubes; modern dimmers won't function with old-style preheat tubes. Then you must replace the ballast (transformer) in the fixture with a special dimming ballast; a wiring diagram for a typical two-wire dimming ballast is shown below left.

It's important to use a two-wire dimming ballast and matching dimmer to avoid having to rewire the run between them with five-wire cable—a difficult chore. Wire the two-wire fluorescent dimmer into the switch box as you would an incandescent dimmer.

REPLACING SURFACE-MOUNTED FIXTURES

Surface-mounted fixtures include both track lights and cord and chain-hung fixtures that connect directly to the ceiling or wall. Most surface-mounted fixtures are relatively easy to replace with a different style. For example, you can readily substitute an elaborate chandelier for a simple ceiling globe. However, track systems often require special installation procedures; see page 91 for more information.

Recessed fixtures are intended to be more permanent than surface-mounted fixtures, and are difficult to exchange; for information on adding recessed fixtures, see page 91.

Single-bar–mounted fixture

Mounting bar

Nipple

Canopy

Tube holder

Knockout hole

Nut

Ballast

Normally, you don't need an electrical permit to exchange fixtures, but it's a good idea to check with your building department in any case.

Weight and grounding considerations

Fixtures usually come with their own mounting hardware, adaptable to any fixture box (two of the most common assemblies are shown below). Sometimes, however, the weight of the new fixture or the wiring necessary to ground it properly requires that you replace the box before attaching the fixture to it.

Fixture weight determines type of attachment. Boxes for fixtures weighing more than 5 pounds must be nailed to a joist or hung on a bar between two joists (see page 89). If the fixture weighs more than 30 pounds, the fixture should be connected to the box's

Pivot-bar–mounted fixture

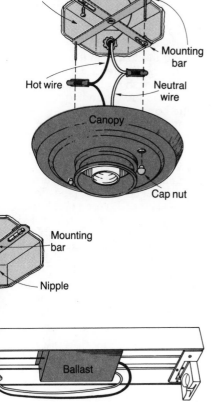

Fixture box

Mounting bar

Hot wire

Neutral wire

Canopy

Cap nut

metallic stud with a hickey or reducing nut (see drawing of a chain-hung fixture below).

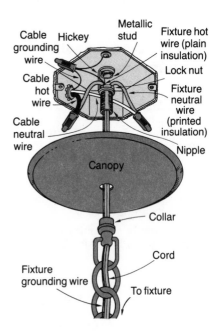

Cable grounding wire
Hickey
Metallic stud
Fixture hot wire (plain insulation)
Lock nut
Cable hot wire
Fixture neutral wire (printed insulation)
Cable neutral wire
Nipple
Canopy
Collar
Cord
Fixture grounding wire
To fixture

Metal fixtures must be grounded.
The National Electrical Code requires that all incandescent and fluorescent fixtures with exposed metal parts must be grounded.

If the fixture box itself is grounded, the nipple or screws holding the fixture to the box will ground the fixture. If the fixture is equipped with a grounding wire, attach it to the grounding terminal in the box.

If the fixture box is not grounded (as is the case when house wiring includes no grounding wire), you'll have to extend a grounding wire from the fixture to the nearest cold-water pipe. To do this, you'll need a length of bare #12 copper wire and a perforated grounding strap (both available at electrical supply dealers). Wrap one end of the copper wire around the nipple or screws holding the fixture to the box, or, if the fixture has its own grounding wire, splice the copper wire to the grounding wire with a wirenut (see page 84).

Extend the copper wire from the box to a cold-water pipe, then wrap the grounding strap around the pipe, and the free end of the wire around the screw that holds the strap to the pipe. Use a nut to secure the wire to the screw.

Basic replacement technique

Whether you're replacing an old fixture with a similar or dissimilar one, the steps are generally the same. In sequence, these steps are:

1) Disconnect the circuit by removing the fuse or switching the circuit breaker to OFF.

2) Carefully remove the glass shade, if any, from the old fixture.

3) Unscrew the canopy from the fixture box, and unscrew the mounting bar if there is one. Have an assistant hold the fixture to keep it from falling, or hang it from the box with a hook made from a wire clothes hanger.

4) Make a sketch of how the wires are connected.

5) If the wires are spliced with wirenuts, unscrew the nuts counterclockwise, then untwist the wires. If the wires are spliced only with electrician's tape, simply unwind the tape; plan to cover new splices with wirenuts. Lay the old fixture aside.

6) Trim the wiring on the new fixture of excess (there's usually some). Strip $1/2$ inch of insulation from the ends of the wires.

7) As an assistant or a wire hanger holds up the new fixture, match its wires to those in the ceiling or wall as shown in your sketch—black to black, white to white. Splice with wirenuts.

8) Secure the new fixture by reversing the steps you took to loosen the original; use a new mounting bar if one is included with the new fixture. If you need to patch the ceiling or wall, see page 90.

ADDING FIX-TURES, PLUG-IN OUTLETS, AND SWITCHES

The following pages cover the general techniques for adding the fixtures, plug-in outlets, and switches described on pages 90–93. (If you plan to use surface

wiring instead of concealed wiring, see page 85.) Installation procedures are the same whether the new fixtures will house incandescent 120-volt or low-voltage bulbs, or fluorescent tubes.

The following sections deal in sequence with the six steps necessary for extending a circuit: selecting an existing housing box (see page 84) as a power source, preparing for one or more new housing boxes, routing new cable from the power source housing box to new housing box locations, attaching new housing boxes, wiring the new cable, and patching the walls or ceiling afterwards.

An electrical permit will probably be required for work on this scale. Be sure to cut off the power before you start work.

Selecting a power source

A circuit can be tapped for power wherever there's a housing box holding a fixture, plug-in outlet, or switch (the exception is a box in which there's no neutral wire, as in the two upper illustrations of switch connections on page 86). The box must be roomy enough to accommodate the additional three wires of the new cable, and must have a knockout hole through which you can thread the new cable; if the most conveniently located old box doesn't fit these requirements, you can replace it with another box.

Before deciding which housing box to tap, consider how you'll route the cable to the new fixture, plug-in outlet, or switch. Take your home's construction into account, and look for the easiest ways to route cable behind walls, above ceilings, and under floors. The best route is one that is direct and accessible, but accessibility is more important than directness. What you'll save in time and effort by avoiding extensive cutting and patching of walls, ceilings, and floors will nearly always offset the added cost of materials for a longer, more indirect cable run.

The most common wall and ceiling covering, gypsum wallboard, is relatively easy to cut away and replace. But avoid cutting into ceramic tile and wood flooring whenever possible.

Preparing for new boxes

After selecting the power source but before routing the cable, you must buy the right boxes, determine where to put them, and cut holes for them in the walls or in the ceiling.

Choosing boxes. Housing boxes come in many types and sizes (see drawing at far right).

For outlets and switches, and for fixtures that weigh 5 pounds or less, choose "cut-in" boxes, which let you secure the box without mounting it to a stud or joist. For fixtures that weigh more than 5 pounds, use boxes that can be nailed to studs or joists.

Unless local regulations prohibit the use of plastic, the choice of metal or plastic boxes is up to you. Metal boxes must be grounded; newly installed plastic boxes cost less and need not be grounded.

Many recessed fixtures come pre-wired to their own housing boxes. For more about these, see page 91.

Selecting box locations. To scout out suitable box locations in a wall or ceiling—to locate the positions not only of studs and joists but also of obstructions such as wires and pipes—first drill a small test hole where you want to put a housing box.

CAUTION: Be sure to cut off power to all circuits that might be wired behind the wall or ceiling before drilling; if you're using a power drill, use an extension cord to connect it to another circuit. Then bend a 9-inch length of stiff wire to a 90° angle at the center, push one side of the angle through the hole, and revolve it. If it bumps into something, you'll probably be able to tell from the feel and sound whether you've hit wood, pipe, or wire. Keep probing until you find a large enough space between joists or studs for installing the box.

Cutting the hole. Once you've found a suitable location for the box, mark the wall or ceiling for cutting the hole. This can be done simply by tracing the basic outline of the box on the wall or ceiling; omit any protruding brackets from your outline.

To cut the box hole, drill a starter hole at one corner of the outline; then use a saber saw or keyhole saw. If you're going to cut through plaster, first tape along the outside border of your outline with masking tape to prevent the plaster from cracking.

Routing new cable

After cutting the holes but *before mounting the boxes,* you must run cable from the power source to each new box location. Clamp one end of each new cable inside the power source box, leaving 8 inches more than you'll need for the connection, before routing the cable. Wait until you have all the new boxes mounted and wired, and all new cable in place, before you make any actual hookups to the source.

Where you have access from a basement with an unfinished ceiling or an attic with no floor, it's easy to run cable either on top of joists or through holes drilled in them.

You'll have to "fish" cable (see drawing below) through walls

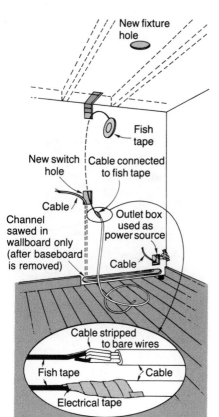

that are covered on both sides. A fish tape (see page 84) is the tool to use for long cable runs. For shorter distances, use a length of stiff wire with one end bent into a tight, blunt hook. Be sure that whatever you use is long enough to span the entire distance plus 2 feet.

Attaching new boxes

After routing new cable, but before connecting it to new fixtures, plug-in outlets, or switches, you'll need to secure each new housing box to the ceiling or wall.

First slip a cable connector onto the end of the cable, then insert the cable through a knockout hole in the box. Fasten the connector to the box, leaving 6 to 8 inches of cable sticking into the box for making connections.

How you should mount the box itself will depend on its type.

Types of housing boxes

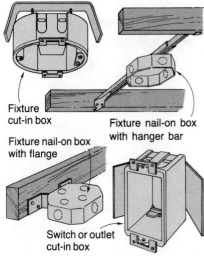

Fixture cut-in box

Fixture nail-on box with hanger bar

Fixture nail-on box with flange

Switch or outlet cut-in box

Cut-in box. Once this type of box is inside the wall or ceiling, its side teeth flare away; tightening the screw at the back of the box pushes the teeth into the back side of the wall or ceiling. Because you can't remove this type of box once it's installed, be sure the cables are in place and the box fits the hole before installing it; to test for fit, remove the box's side teeth.

Box attached to studs or joists. Three types of boxes attach to wall studs or ceiling joists. One type has a hanger bar that spans the space between two studs or joists. Another has a flange that attaches to the side of a single joist. The third type, designed for recessed fixtures, is shown on page 91. All three types are nailed into place.

Wiring new cable

Once all new boxes are mounted, you can wire in the new cable. Connections to the three different kinds of boxes used as power sources are shown on this page. Typical connections from new boxes to new fixtures are on page 91, to new plug-in outlets on pages 92–93, and to new switches on pages 93–94.

Before screwing the cover plate onto any new box, you'll want to be sure that your wiring connections were made correctly; use a neon voltage tester, as explained on page 84. Because you must first turn the current back on to test connections, be very careful to grasp only the insulated portions of the tester while using it.

Patching walls and ceilings

Finally, you'll no doubt want to make the walls or ceilings you've cut into look like new.

Patching gypsum wallboard. For small repairs, use a broad-blade

putty knife and spackling compound.

Larger holes may require fitting with a new piece of wallboard cut to fit around the new box. If there are no studs or joists to which you can nail the piece, glue some small blocks of wood behind the hole so that their edges protrude into the hole. When the glue has dried, shape a piece of wallboard to fit the hole, and glue it to the wood blocks. If you nail a new piece in place, dimple the surface at the nail heads, then spread joint compound across the dimples.

With joint tape and compound, cover the joints between the new piece and the surrounding surface. Spread a layer of compound over the tape; let dry.

Apply a second coat of compound to the nail heads and tape, feathering the edges of the first coat. Sand all nail dimples and joints when dry, and paint.

Patching plaster. For patching small gaps, use a broad-blade putty knife to apply commercial plaster compound.

For larger holes, you'll first have to provide some kind of backing, such as lath; clean and moisten the edges of the hole; and, sometimes, apply more than one coat of patching compound.

When the patching compound has dried, sand and paint.

ADDING SURFACE-MOUNTED FIXTURES

Adding a surface-mounted fixture is much like replacing one (see page 87) but the incoming house wiring will always include a grounding wire that must be attached to the box for an added fixture.

Common ways of attaching a surface-mounted fixture to its box (whether a replacement or new installation) are illustrated on pages 87–88.

Whatever kind of work you're doing, don't forget to turn OFF the power to the circuit you're dealing with before starting.

Grounding the box. Fixture boxes come equipped with a grounding screw. In metallic boxes the screw is often green; in any case, it should have the code "G" or "Gr" stamped near it. In plastic boxes the screw threads into a small metal bar.

With nonmetallic sheathed cable (and other types of cable), you can identify the grounding wire, which must be attached to the grounding screw, in one of three ways: the wire will be 1)

Fixture box as power source

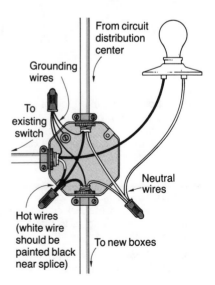

Outlet box as power source

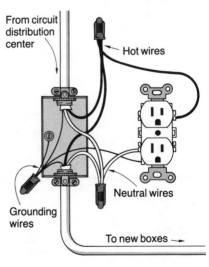

Switch box as power source

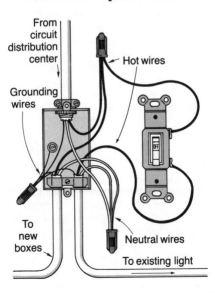

bare, 2) spiral-wrapped in paper, or 3) covered in green plastic.

If only one cable enters the box, wrap the bare end of its grounding wire around the grounding screw in a clockwise direction, and tighten the screw. If more than one cable enters the box, you'll need to wrap the bare end of a short length of #12 bare or green insulated wire under the grounding screw, and twist its other end with the ends of the grounding wires. Cap the twisted ends of the wires with a wirenut.

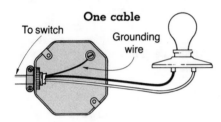

One cable

To switch
Grounding wire

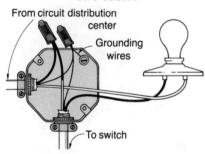

Two cables

From circuit distribution center
Grounding wires
To switch

Flush-mounted and cord or chain-hung fixtures. A fixture mounted flush with a wall or ceiling on a grounded box is automatically grounded to the box by the mounting screws or nipple. A fixture hanging from a cord or chain needs a grounding wire run from the socket to the box, as shown on page 88. Most cord or chain-hung fixtures are prewired with a grounding wire; if you need to install your own, use #12 wire.

ADDING RECESSED FIXTURES

Recessed fixtures fall into two categories; both types are easy to install. One type wires into a hous-

ing box that's been nailed to a joist beforehand; the other comes pre-wired and grounded to its own housing box.

Cutting the ceiling hole. Before installing the fixture, you'll need to cut a hole for the fixture housing in the ceiling between two joists. If there's no crawl space above the joists, find the joists (and any obstructing wires or pipes) from below by the bent-wire method described on page 89; don't forget to turn off power to any circuits that might be wired behind the ceiling before drilling exploratory holes.

Once you've located a suitable place for it, trace the outline of the fixture housing on the ceiling with a pencil; use a keyhole saw or saber saw for cutting the necessary hole.

Installing a fixture sold with a box. This type of fixture and its box are premounted on a metal frame that 1) slips through the hole cut in the ceiling and 2) clips to the ceiling edges as shown. The fixture housing then 3) snaps into its socket and into the frame.

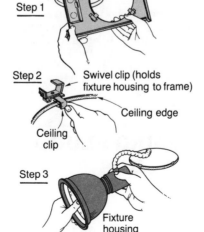

Housing box
Fixture's metal-clad cable
Ceiling clip
Metal frame
Socket

Step 1

Step 2
Swivel clip (holds fixture housing to frame)
Ceiling edge
Ceiling clip

Step 3
Fixture housing

Installing a fixture sold without a box. To link this type of fixture with incoming cable, it's important first to select a housing box whose back can be nailed to a joist, as shown. The metal-clad ("flex") cable of the fixture grounds the fixture to the box when inserted into it.

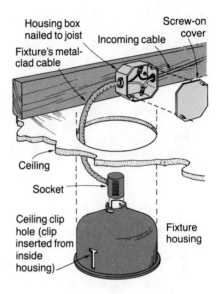

Housing box nailed to joist
Screw-on cover
Incoming cable
Fixture's metal-clad cable
Ceiling
Socket
Ceiling clip hole (clip inserted from inside housing)
Fixture housing

INSTALLING TRACK SYSTEMS

With track systems you can add lighting fixtures in a variety of locations without having to install an equal number of new boxes. Wiring in a track with two or more circuits is a job best left to a professional electrician.

Where to place the track

Where you should install a track will depend on where you can connect the new system into a power source.

Plug-in versus wire-in connections. A plug-in connector, consisting of a 12-foot cord and lamp plug, lets you place a track wherever the cord will reach a plug-in outlet. Plug-in connectors, however, are only available with single-circuit tracks.

A track system with a wire-in connector is hooked up directly to a fixture box. You may be able to use a box already installed (see page 87), or you may have to install a new one (see page 88). Either way, you'll need as many wall switches as your track has circuits. If you're simply replacing a fixture with a single-circuit track system, you can use the wall switch that's already wired to the old fixture's box.

Bringing power to the track

Once you've decided what power source to use and added the necessary switches (see page 93), it's time to attach the track connector to the ceiling or wall. By using a special connector available with some track systems, you can bring power in along a track run rather than at the end.

Mounting the track

For attaching a track or mounting clips to the ceiling or wall, plan to use screws or toggle bolts in predrilled holes.

To lay out and drill the necessary holes, line up a chalk line or the edge of a yardstick with the center slot of the connector, and snap or draw a line to where the track will end (if you use a yardstick, move it along as necessary). Setting a length of track beside the line, mark along the line the positions of the knockout holes located in the roof of the track—these marks will indicate where to drill holes for attaching the track or its clips.

Mounting a plug-in track. Because a plug-in connector attaches directly against the mounting surface, you can also attach the track directly against the ceiling or wall without having to use mounting clips. Slip the two bare wire ends of the first length of track into the connector receptacles, then secure the track with screws or toggle bolts. Proceed in a similar manner with the remaining lengths of track.

Mounting a wire-in track. Since a wire-in connector holds the end of the track ¼ to ½ inch away from the mounting surface, you need

Plug-in connection to track

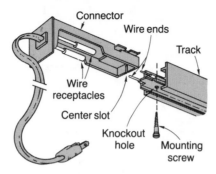

Wire-in connection to a single-circuit track

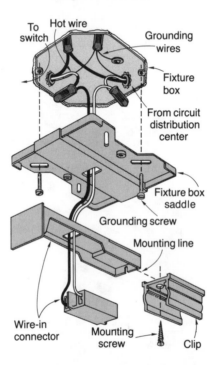

special clips to keep the rest of the track level. Once these clips are screwed or bolted to the ceiling or wall, slip the first length of track into the connector, and press it and succeeding lengths into the clips.

ADDING PLUG-IN OUTLETS

Plug-in outlets can be wired in several ways. You may wish to have one or both halves electrically live at all times so that

you can control plug-in lamps by their own switches. Or you may wish to be able to turn one or both halves ON and OFF so that you can control lamps with wall switches.

The illustrations below and at the top of the next page show three common ways of attaching cable to new plug-in outlets. The outlet boxes are presumed to be metal; if you use plastic boxes, there's no need to ground the boxes themselves, but do attach a grounding wire to each outlet by looping the end of the wire under the grounding screw.

You'll need to break off the little "ear" between brass screws when one half of the outlet is to be controlled by a wall switch.

Both halves always hot

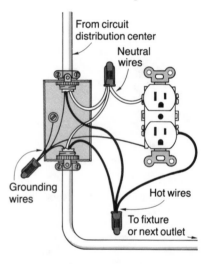

Bottom half always hot, top half controlled by wall switch

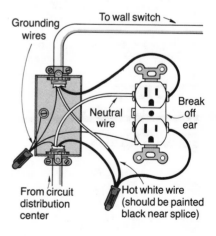

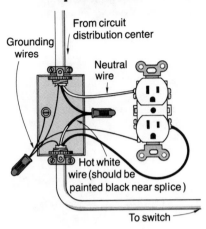

Both halves controlled by wall switch

From circuit distribution center

Grounding wires

Neutral wire

Hot white wire (should be painted black near splice)

To switch

ADDING SWITCHES

Most switches in a home are either single-pole or three-way. With a single-pole switch, one switch controls one or more light fixtures or plug-in outlets. With a three-way switch, two switches in different locations both control one or more fixtures or outlets. Certain rules of thumb apply to both types.

General guidelines

When shopping for switches, be sure to read carefully the information stamped on the new switch. The switch must have the same amp and voltage rating as the circuit you plan to tap into (you'll find the circuit rating on the circuit's fuse or circuit breaker handle in the circuit distribution center—see page 82). If your house's wiring is aluminum, also be sure that the switch is designed to be used with aluminum wire—if it is, it will be identified by the letters CU-AL.

When doing the wiring, the most important concept to remember is that *switches are installed only along hot wires.*

You'll notice that the switches shown on this page have no grounding wires connected to them. Because the plastic toggles used on most home switches are

shockproof, the switches do not need grounding.

Wiring single-pole switches

Single-pole switches have two screw terminals of the same color (usually brass) for wire connections, and a definite right side up—you should be able to read the words "ON" and "OFF" embossed on the toggle. It makes no difference which hot wire goes to which terminal. Because of code limitations on the number of wires that a switch box may contain,

Single-pole switch wiring if power enters switch box

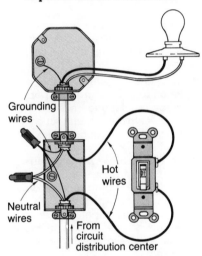

Grounding wires

Neutral wires

Hot wires

From circuit distribution center

Single-pole switch wiring if power enters fixture box

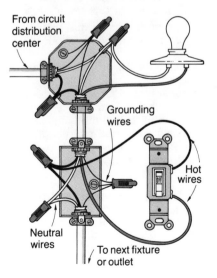

From circuit distribution center

Grounding wires

Neutral wires

Hot wires

To next fixture or outlet

circuit distribution panel wires sometimes run to the fixture, and sometimes to the switch.

Wiring three-way switches

Three-way switches have two screw terminals of the same color (brass or silver) and one of a darker color, identified by the word "common." Though a three-way switch has no right side up, it's important to observe which of the three terminals is the odd-colored one; it may be located in a different place from that shown on the switches illustrated below and on the next page.

To wire a pair of three-way switches, connect the hot wire from the circuit distribution panel to the odd-colored terminal of one switch; connect the hot wire from the fixture to the odd-colored terminal of the other switch. Then wire the four remaining terminals by running two hot wires between the two same-colored terminals on one and the two same-colored terminals on the other.

Three-way switch wiring if power enters switch box

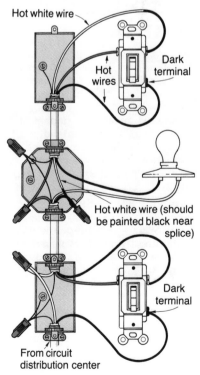

Hot white wire

Hot wires

Dark terminal

Hot white wire (should be painted black near splice)

Dark terminal

From circuit distribution center

Three-way switch wiring if power enters fixture box

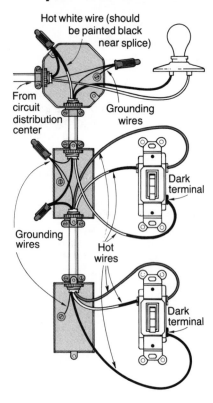

Hot white wire (should be painted black near splice)

From circuit distribution center

Grounding wires

Grounding wires

Hot wires

Dark terminal

Dark terminal

ADDING OUTDOOR LIGHTS

Whether its purpose is to highlight plantings and structures, discourage prowlers, or light pathways and recreation areas, outdoor lighting is a welcome addition to any house. You can extend your home's 120-volt system into the garden with a variety of permanently placed fixtures, or step the system down to 12 volts with lighter-weight fixtures that can be easily moved.

If you're thinking of adding outdoor lights to an existing circuit, see "Calculating maximum watts" on page 83. If you need to add a circuit, consult an electrician or refer to the *Sunset* book *Basic Home Wiring Illustrated*.

For placement ideas and help with design, see pages 78–79. Security considerations are discussed on page 12.

Taking wiring outdoors

The techniques for extending wiring to the outside are much the same as those used for extending it indoors (see page 88). The only difference is that an outdoor housing box must be waterproof. This is true whether it contains a plug-in outlet for a 12-volt transformer or simply space for splicing 120-volt indoor wiring to 120-volt outdoor wiring.

12 volts or 120 volts?

Once you've brought your 120-volt indoor wiring to a waterproof housing box outdoors, you'll need to decide whether to add an outlet for a 12-volt transformer or to splice in 120-volt outdoor wiring.

12-volt system. Here are some reasons why you may wish to install a 12-volt (often called a "low-voltage") system:

● Installation is simple: cable can lie on top of the ground, perhaps hidden by foliage; most fixtures connect to cables without wirenuts; and no grounding hookups are required.

● No electrical permit is required for installing a system that extends from a plug-in transformer (the most common type).

● There is no danger that people or pets will get a harmful shock from low-voltage fixtures or wiring.

120-volt system. A 120-volt outdoor lighting system has these advantages:

● The buried cable and metallic fixtures give the installation a look of permanence.

● Light can be projected a great distance—especially useful for security and for lighting trees from the ground.

● In addition to light fixtures, power tools and patio heaters can be plugged into 120-volt outdoor outlets.

Adding a 12-volt system

To install a 12-volt system, you'll need a transformer, up to four 100-foot runs of 2-wire outdoor cable, and a set of 12-volt fixtures.

To activate the system, you'll need to connect the transformer, and perhaps a separate switching device, to an existing power source.

Wire thickness. Most low-voltage outdoor fixtures use stranded wire cable. What size the wires in the cable should be will depend on the aggregate wattage of the fixtures to be served. Here are the appropriate sizes for some typical wattages:

#14 wire—up to 144 watts at 12 volts
#12 wire—up to 192 watts at 12 volts
#10 wire—up to 288 watts at 12 volts

Types of transformers. Transformers designed for low-voltage outdoor lighting are mounted outdoors in weathertight boxes; they have three-pronged (grounded) plugs that are inserted into already installed three-hole grounded outdoor outlets, or into shockproof outlets called "ground fault circuit interrupters" (see "Installing a transformer," following).

Most transformers are rated for home use from 100 to 300 watts. The rating shows the total allowable wattage of the fixtures serviced. The higher the rating, the more lengths of 100-foot cable—up to a total of four—the transformer can supply power through; each length extends like a spoke from the transformer.

Selecting a transformer that has a built-in timing device or ON-OFF switch (some models have both) will relieve you of having to wire in a separate switch.

Installing a transformer. Most transformers for outdoor lights are encased in watertight boxes; but to be safe, plan to install yours at least a foot off the ground in a sheltered location.

If you don't already have an outlet into which to plug the transformer, plan to use instead a ground fault circuit interrupter (abbreviated GFCI or GFI). Like an outlet, this device accepts a standard three-pronged plug, but also cuts off power within $1/40$ of a second if current begins leaking anywhere along the circuit. The drawing at right shows how to wire an outdoor GFCI; see page 88 for ways to tap into an existing power source.

Though many transformers have built-in switches, some do not. Installing a separate switch indoors will probably prove more convenient than installing it outside. The drawing at right shows how to wire a new indoor switch and existing power source to a new GFCI.

To connect one or more low-voltage cables to the transformer, simply wrap the two bare wire ends of each length of cable clockwise around the terminal screws on the transformer—if the transformer accommodates more than one cable, the terminal screws will come in pairs—and tighten the screws. Which wire connects to which screw in each pairing makes no difference.

Ground fault circuit interrupter (GFCI)

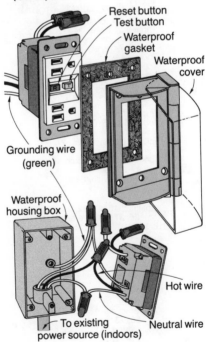

Reset button
Test button
Waterproof gasket
Waterproof cover
Grounding wire (green)
Waterproof housing box
Hot wire
To existing power source (indoors)
Neutral wire

Connecting fixtures to the cable.

Once your transformer is in place, and you've decided where to put the fixtures, you'll need to hook them into the cable or cables leading from the transformer.

With some fixtures, you simply pierce the cable with a screwdown connector already attached

to the rear of the fixture. With others, you must screw an unattached connector to the main cable and to the end of a short cable leading from the fixture. Neither of these types of connector requires removing insulation from the cable.

A few brands of fixtures require splicing into the main cable with wirenuts (see page 84). Use plastic housing boxes to insulate splices that can't be pushed back into the fixtures.

Wiring an indoor switch and power source to new GFCI

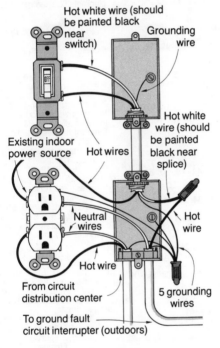

Hot white wire (should be painted black near switch)
Grounding wire
Existing indoor power source
Hot wires
Hot white wire (should be painted black near splice)
Neutral wires
Hot wire
From circuit distribution center
Hot wire
5 grounding wires
To ground fault circuit interrupter (outdoors)

Adding a 120-volt system

To install a 120-volt outdoor system, you'll need a set of fixtures, of course, and some weatherproof 120-volt cable (if allowed by local code) or conduit—either can be of unlimited length. To activate the system, you'll probably want to hook an indoor switch and timer into an existing power source.

Installing an indoor switch and timer.

By wiring in a switch and a timer as shown in the drawing at right, you can turn outdoor lights on and off by hand or let the timer do it for you whether you're at home or away.

Wiring an indoor switch and timer for 120-volt outdoor fixtures

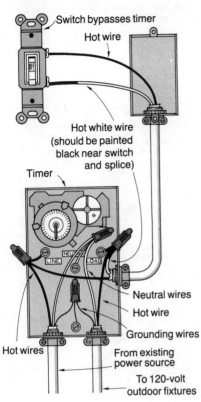

Switch bypasses timer
Hot wire
Hot white wire (should be painted black near switch and splice)
Timer
Neutral wires
Hot wire
Grounding wires
Hot wires
From existing power source
To 120-volt outdoor fixtures

Types of outdoor cable and conduit.

Most local electrical codes allow the use of rigid conduit for outdoor wiring. Plastic conduit, though lighter and less expensive than steel, must be buried at least 18 inches underground. Steel conduit can be buried as little as 1 inch underground. Run two #14 thermoplastic-insulated (TW) wires through steel conduit, which is self-grounding; three TW #14 wires (including a ground wire) through plastic. For details about working with conduit, see the Sunset book Basic Home Wiring Illustrated.

Some local codes allow the use of three-wire UF (underground feeder) flexible cable instead of rigid conduit. UF cable must be buried at least 18 inches underground. Work with UF cable in the same way you work with nonmetallic sheathed cable (see page 84). Before covering the cable with dirt, lay a redwood board on top of it so that you won't accidentally spade through it at a later time.

INDEX

Boldface numbers refer to color photographs.